IN THE IMAGE OF SAINT DOMINIC

GUY BEDOUELLE, O.P.

IN THE IMAGE
OF
SAINT DOMINIC

Nine Portraits of Dominican Life

∾

Translated by
Sr. Mary Thomas Noble, O.P.
With original sources translated by
W. Becket Soule, O.P.

Foreword by
TIMOTHY RADCLIFFE, O.P.

IGNATIUS PRESS   SAN FRANCISCO

Cover art: Fra Angelico, *Crucifixion with
the Virgin and Saints John the Evangelist,
Dominic, and Thomas Aquinas* (detail),
S. Marco, Florence, Italy
Scala/Art Resource, New York

Cover design by Roxanne Mei Lum

ISBN 978-0-89870-467-9
Library of Congress Control Number 93-78534
Printed in the United States of America ∞

CONTENTS

Foreword 7

Introduction:
Nine Ways of Dominican Life 13

1. Jordan of Saxony, and Concern for the
   Dominican Communion 19

   — return to the essential —

2. Saint Peter of Verona: The Burden of a
   Heritage 31

   — the armor of light —

3. Saint Thomas Aquinas and the Search for
   Truth 45

   — study —

4. Saint Catherine of Siena and Love for the
   Church 59

   — prayer —

5. Fra Angelico: Preaching through Beauty . . . 71

   — art —

6. Las Casas and the Struggle for Justice 89

— *indignation* —

7. Saint Catherine de Ricci and the Mystical
   Dimension of the Dominican Life 103

— *spiritual realism* —

8. Saint Martin de Porres: Humility and Love
   of the Poor 115

— *poverty* —

9. Lacordaire, or the Defense of Liberty 127

— *friendship* —

Conclusion:
Saint Dominic and Fervor 141

— *joy* —

Postscript 159

Bibliography 161

FOREWORD

After nearly eight centuries we Dominicans are still one Order, while enjoying that diversity of gifts which, according to St. Paul, is a sign of the working of the Holy Spirit (1 Cor 12:12–30). Given the Order's active involvement, since the thirteenth century, in most of the important events that have marked the history of the Church and society, this unity is astonishing. Yet it is this unity that St. Dominic prayed might bind together his followers.

Just think how different are the circumstances in which one might have encountered a Dominican during this long history, marked by both continuity and contrast. In the thirteenth century one might have come across a couple of the brethren making their way across the country lanes of Europe, singing psalms to keep up their spirits, in danger of attack by thieves or heretics, on their way to the frontiers of Christendom and beyond. Or one might have found them preaching in our churches built in the new towns that were appearing all over Europe at that time, teaching in the newly founded universities such as Paris and Oxford, debating the hot issues of the day, the suspect Aristotelian philosophy or the new experimental sciences, and even experimenting with a little alchemy. During the Renaissance these same churches are transformed by the artists and architects of the time, such as Botticelli in Florence or da Vinci in Milan, and are where the brethren struggle with the new questions of the moment, St. Antoninus wrestling with the moral problems posed by the new world economy or Francisco de Vitoria engaged in the first formulation of a theory of human rights. Other brethren cross the Atlantic in search of a new world, and disappear into the jungles of Central America, refusing the protection of the armies so as to preach peacefully to the native people. In the last century we find the brethren again crossing the ocean, in the new steamships, to accompany their people as they push west in search of food and gold and freedom. In our own age, the followers of St. Dominic are to be found nearly everywhere—ninety-two countries sent representatives to the General Chapter of 1992 in Mexico—engaged in every imaginable work, from running an ecological farm in Benin to exploring Coptic verbs in Fribourg. What has held all these different men and women together throughout the ages? A passion for the gospel, after the image of St. Dominic.

As one reads these fascinating pages by Father Guy Bedouelle, one is constantly struck by how many of the people whom he describes are marked by a passion and a fervor. It may be the passionate intellectual search of St. Thomas, who asked of Jesus: "*Non nisi te, Domine*" ("Nothing but you, Lord"), or Bartolomé de Las Casas, vigorously pursuing justice for the Indians:

"I believe God wants me to fill heaven and earth and the whole earth anew, with cries, tears and groans!", as he wrote to the King. Or there is St. Catherine of Siena, with her "sweet, loving, grieving desires" for the reform of her Church, and who reverenced the Christ who was in the center of her being as love and desire. In all this passion we see both various expressions of that fervor which so marked St. Dominic, and the many faceted attraction of the God who would draw us to Himself by touching our deepest desires.

Recent General Chapters have tried to help the Order focus its priorities in face of such endless demands and possibilities. In particular our apostolic commitment aims to achieve four main objectives: intellectual formation, world mission, social communication, and justice. Because of the place our brother Thomas Aquinas holds in the Church, few will be surprised that the pursuit of Truth and the sanctification of the human intelligence is one of our priorities. This is a searching which God may grace. And despite, within contemporary Western culture, a profound suspicion of "arid intellectualism", all true study is deeply pastoral. Justice cannot flourish in a society that does not nurture a passion for Truth for its own sake and not for what it may yield financially. And careful attention to texts can be a wonderful training for an attentive, patient listening to other people! The greatest scholars I have known have been people of deep pastoral instincts. And so it is not surprising that our study carried us to the frontiers of the apostolic life, as happened in the case of the thirteenth century martyr Peter of Verona, the form of whose dedication we may have to struggle a little to understand. Or in the contrasting case of Henri-Dominique Lacordaire in the nineteenth century, we see a man engaged in the frontiers between the gospel and a world of predominantly secular values, seeking to understand anew the nature of liberty.

As preachers of the Gospel, Dominicans must wrestle with the arts of communication. Today this calls for every resource that science can supply, but even before the age of the mass media, of television and radio, Dominicans included men and women who had a remarkable ability to gain other people's attention: saints of the fourteenth century such as the blessed Fra Angelico, whose depictions of the mysteries of Christ's life still captivate us, or the uneducated saint, Catherine of Siena, whose dialogues with God and letters to ordinary people can still enchant and challenge us today. And what about the communication skills of my thirteenth century predecessor Blessed Jordan of Saxony, of whom it was said that parents locked up their children when he came to preach lest they not be seen again!

The preached word does not merely communicate an abstract truth but can refashion lives and society. If it is in any sense "the Word of the Lord", then it is a creative and transforming word, helping to bring about the Kingdom. And so there is a deep relationship between the Dominican vocation to preach, and a passion for justice. And so, among the many Dominicans from both the old and the new worlds that one could cite, it is especially pleasing that the present volume includes the example of a woman and a cleric and a cooperator brother, each of whom represents this passion for a more just world. In Renaissance Italy, the cloistered nun and mystic, St. Catherine de Ricci, graciously yet firmly withstood the insistence of certain ecclesiastical authorities who failed to appreciate the *souplesse* required to maintain a viable religious life for the women of her day. And of course there is Bartolomé de Las Casas whose championing of the full rights of the native American peoples remains a beacon for us today. Then half a century later, we have the extraordinary witness of the mulatto cooperator brother, St. Martin de Porres, who cheerfully demonstrated to the Church of the new world the fire of charity that the Gospel can ignite in the midst of terrible suffering.

We need to learn from our brothers and sisters some of their courage and passion. May they help us to have the nerve to let ourselves be touched at the heart of our being by the God who would seduce us, if we would but let him. So, at the beginning of my term of Master of the Order of Friars Preachers, it gives me great pleasure to present Father Guy Bedouelle's collection of essays and original sources, which so beautifully captures the life and spirit of the Dominican Family. Those who have already profited from his *Saint Dominic: The Grace of the Word* will find this new volume equally rewarding. And for those who are learning about the Dominican Order for the first time, these pages will provide an irresistible invitation to discover more.

TIMOTHY RADCLIFFE, O.P.
Master of the Order of Friars Preachers

INTRODUCTION:
NINE WAYS OF DOMINICAN LIFE

T HE MOST SUBLIME IDEAS need to be enfleshed. The most generous ideal must be incarnate. It is the gift of founders, such as St. Dominic, St. Francis, and St. Ignatius, to present in a concrete, living, historical way an image of some great ideal of service to the Church. It is very true that St. Dominic, of whom I love to speak, effaced himself behind his work, especially its institutionalization, but also behind his brethren, in his own day as well as in history. This is what I should like to prove, by showing that the spirit of St. Dominic—an expression preferable to "Dominican spirituality"—can only be fully understood in his posterity, and particularly in the saints recognized by the Church. To do this, I shall take nine examples, well aware that there could be so many others.

Why nine ways of Dominican life? Of course I am inspired by *The Nine Ways of Prayer of St. Dominic*, that short spiritual work produced in the Dominican milieu of Bologna in the second half of the thirteenth century, between 1260 and 1288. What is interesting is that St. Dominic's love of prayer, attested by all the depositions at his process of canonization as well as in his first biography, the *Libellus* of Jordan of Saxony, takes on visible, physical, representable forms, and this is why many manuscripts of this small work are so often illustrated by miniatures. In them, St. Dominic's prayer becomes an art in which the body, the voice, gestures all have their place and are associated with very definite memories of his companions, gathered by Tradition. I think this can be compared to the richness of the Dominican charism that has unfolded through time, that is, for nearly eight centuries. What we find in the appealing figure of our Founder, in our men and women saints and blesseds and also, happily, in each one of us, combines to give body, style, voice, a way of being that is unique and reveals different facets of this charism. We all grow richer in the sharing of it.

Thus we see in our first century, the thirteenth, how Blessed Jordan of Saxony concretely built concern for communion among Dominican brethren and sisters, thereby creating a profound unity in a single Order of Preachers. We see St. Peter of Verona, converted from Catharism, struggling as an Inquisitor for the integrity of the Faith; St. Thomas Aquinas, a Doctor of the Church, searching for truth in study and teaching throughout his life. Then there is Fra Angelico, an artist indeed who preached through the beauty of his paintings and who also bore the responsibility of government in his province. Soon after came St. Catherine of Siena, dedicating her life of prayer and action to the love of the Church, whose members, in her day, were dividing, opposing, and destroying one another. In the sixteenth century we see Bartolomé de las Casas, concerned with the new world in which Europeans who had come to bleed and even devastate it were profiteering and ravaging. He proclaimed with indignation that evangelization was the first duty of the Church, which could only be accomplished with true justice. In Italy St. Catherine de Ricci, a contemporary of St. Teresa of Avila, had extraordinary mystical experiences and recalls to us the contemplative dimension so necessary to Dominican life. At the same time she maintained a profound realism. Then in Peru, together with St. John Macias and St. Rose of Lima, St. Martin de Porres, a mulatto cooperator brother, shows us that there is indeed a place for humility in the Dominican Order, and he teaches us how our vow of poverty can be translated into service of the poor. Finally, in the nineteenth century Lacordaire, restorer of the Order in France—where it had been suppressed by the Revolution—brought to the fore the ideal of liberty so dear to modern Dominicans, a liberty rooted in the theological insight in which love for God and friendship between all men presupposes a responsible exercise of free choice. These are the manifold values rendered present to us in the course of the centuries, which I should like to show revealed in St. Dominic either explicitly or implicitly in his posterity. We could certainly have talked about the Rhineland mystics, St. Vincent Ferrer, Savonarola, Pius V, and many others, but I had to choose.

Canonized saints call for imitation because they imitated Christ—indeed, this is why they were canonized.

We try to imitate the virtues our saints propose to us. But it is important to understand what this means, for the history of the Church and of our Order proves that even the most splendid virtues can be disfigured by a too human and narrow view. The search for truth, or zeal for the Faith, can become fanaticism. Friendship can assume forms that are too human and lead to cliques or pressure groups. Our beloved Dominican liberty may become carnal, as St. Paul says. Collaboration with the sisters and the laity can assume purely superficial forms. The search for beauty, the love of art, can be transformed into aestheticism. The struggle for justice may become mere ideology. We have to bear in mind that while Dominican life is many faceted, it must always seek balance, which alone can give it its theological dimension, its depth of faith, hope, and above all charity, which embraces all and gives the fervor of the Spirit.

This is why it is not without profit to study with care and affection these classical portraits of our ancestors in order to discern their holiness beneath the historically incarnated forms of their Dominican destinies. We shall do this with the objective of finding our own path and what Dominican life can bring as a new development for our times, one consonant with the charism of the Order and standing in its full light. Perhaps we can begin by asking our saints to enlighten us in this undertaking, using the words with which Simon Tugwell concluded his English edition of *The Nine Ways of Prayer of Saint Dominic*:

May Saint Dominic himself be with us and pray for us, as he promised, and that great galaxy of saints in his family: Blessed Jordan of Saxony, Fra Angelico, St. Thomas, St. Vincent Ferrer, Catherine of Siena, Martin de Porres and his friend John Macias, Henry Suso, Grignion de Montfort.... A motley crew, united in the love of God, and in the yearning for the salvation of men. May they inspire us and help us, that we too may be a light to the world, a city set on a hill that cannot be hidden! Amen.

JORDAN OF SAXONY, AND CONCERN FOR THE DOMINICAN COMMUNION

IT IS NOT ENOUGH TO FOUND, to set in motion, to start a work; the work must endure, survive. St. Dominic, after years of trial, years of waiting and of humble, small beginnings, came to realize that God wanted him to found a new Order in the Church. Its task would be the renewal of preaching by way of giving an example to those responsible for preaching in the Church, the bishops. He neglected nothing to ensure that this work would succeed valiantly. He achieved its protection by papal documents. He gave it laws both firm and flexible, which combined solidity of past experience with openness for new answers. He knew enough friars had joined him that he could continue to pour life into his foundations already spread throughout Europe.

But what would be the use of all this if a head were lacking, someone to animate, coordinate, arbitrate, settle problems, choose options, resolve possible or inevitable confrontations? A founder has to be on the lookout for a successor, not someone like himself but someone who will be able to steer the same ship through other storms. The rightness of St. Dominic's concern to find a successor is well illustrated by the difficulties encountered by the Franciscan Order a decade later, when it became necessary to replace St. Francis of Assisi, and no person could be found who possessed his many charisms.

St. Dominic's successor was Jordan of Saxony, deliberately chosen by him, a man with enough breadth of mind, dynamism, and fervor to govern the Order for fifteen years before drowning in a ship-wreck off the coast of Syria on his way home from the Holy Land in 1237.

Dominic immediately saw the potential for leadership in this German from the Rhineland. Already a Master at the University of Paris, Jordan was relatively seasoned when he became a Dominican novice, as compared to the young boys he himself was to welcome into the Order.[1] Less than a year later, still a newcomer in the Order, he was appointed Provincial of Lombardy—at the insistence of St. Dominic we may be sure, since he was to succeed him as Master of the Order in 1222. He then set out on a life of active preaching among young university students; he visited new foundations and other convents already more

[1] Letter 48 to Diana d'Andalo.

firmly established and met and brought spiritual help to vast numbers of people.

Jordan is an outstanding example of concern for Dominican communion. I prefer this expression to "the Dominican family" as being more theological, more ecclesial, and doubtless less vague, even though the term *family* was adopted by our Constitutions to describe the bonds uniting the brethren, nuns, active sisters, and laity attached to the Order of St. Dominic. Jordan spent a great deal of time in this task and showed much interest and patience.

There are two irrefutable proofs of this left to us in writing, one of them composed with art and destined to endure, the other drafted with a free spontaneity.

The first of these texts is, obviously, the *Libellus*, which treats the beginnings of the Order of Preachers. We have to see this composition as motivated by a desire to give a common point of reference to all the brethren and also all the sisters who would come to seek their roots in the spirit of St. Dominic "in order to imitate the charity of the first days".[2] This book, one of the gems of medieval hagiography, was ignored for centuries, until Lacordaire's intuition and his sense of the authentic reinstated it. In studying it, I never cease to marvel at the keenness of penetration, the theological sense rooted in a knowledge of Scripture that shines through every sentence, the precision of details gathered from those

[2]No. 3.

who created the Order with St. Dominic. But if we appreciate the historical precision that, for example, assigns to Diego of Osma a key role in the beginnings of the preaching in Languedoc, we are touched by the warm and natural way in which Jordan speaks of his very dear friend Henry of Cologne—the man he swore he would never be separated from but with whom, as it turned out, he never lived!

This familiar, affectionate tone, affective without ever being sentimental, is found again in the *Letters* of direction, or better, of "consolation", addressed to the young nun in the monastery of St. Agnes in Bologna, Diana d'Andalo, a strong personality, quite capable of overcoming every obstacle in her path in order to become a Dominican. But these letters of Jordan—for we possess more of his than of Diana's—witness to the strong bond between the brethren and the sisters, which led to the sharing and circulating of information. It is well known that our cloistered sisters are extremely well informed; I have often received phone calls from prioresses of Dominican monasteries asking me to confirm something I was really unaware of but that turned out to be true! But Jordan's solicitude for the nuns is historically important because shortly thereafter, and for a period of fifty years in the middle of the thirteenth century, the brethren struggled to be free of the spiritual and material care of the sisters, and this situation lasted until the compromise of 1267. At the time of his writing, Jordan, on the contrary, assures

Diana d'Andalo of the assistance of the Dominican brothers[3] and transmits to her the guarantee of this given by the Pope himself.[4] However, the relationship between the brethren and the sisters is primarily a spiritual one.

Jordan repeatedly begs for the sisters' prayers for his "fishing schemes" for the university students whom he wants to draw into the Order. Thus he tells Diana of his "good catches" at the universities of Paris, Oxford, and Padua.[5] Thirty-three brothers entered in 1223[6] and seventy-two in 1234.[7] He constantly gives her news of the Order: there are three letters about the death of Henry of Cologne in 1225; another describes the famous Most General Chapter of 1228;[8] he keeps her up to date on the first confrontations between the seculars and mendicants;[9] he rejoices with her over the canonization of St. Dominic, which strengthens the unity of the Order.[10] At times his letters take on a more personal tone: he asks for news of Diana's family, for the brethren at Bologna were much indebted to the d'Andalos.[11] He sends greetings from "your brother and son, Gerard",

[3] Letter 29.
[4] Letter 21.
[5] Letter 32.
[6] Letter 5.
[7] Letter 48.
[8] Letter 29.
[9] Letter 30.
[10] Letter 47.
[11] Letter 13.

his socius on his journeys. He rejoices when sisters receive the Dominican habit; he is anxious about the little details of daily life. For example, he says, "Know that I suffer in your injured foot."[12]

The tone is even, but his affection is shown unhesitatingly, even though Jordan has to temper the anxieties of his sister in Bologna. "What would you do if I died? ... If I die, do not yield to inconsolable grief, for I shall be of more use to you when I am living with the Lord than when I am dying daily in this world."[13] Here we see Jordan echoing for his sisters Dominic's legacy to his brethren before his death, *O spem miram*.

Again, Jordan never ceases to lead his correspondent, and with her all the community of St. Agnes, to the very heart of Dominican communion: the sisters exercise a ministry of aiding the preaching of their brothers—they implore the protection of the Lord. We come, for example, upon this sentence in which we can see ourselves: "I do not pray much: that is why you must exhort your sisters to make it up for me with their prayer."[14]

And yet again, he always leads Diana and her sisters to the essential: the increase of charity and the other virtues[15] drawn from contemplation of the book of the Cross, the book of life, of charity, "written by Jesus Christ with his wounds and illuminated with

[12] Letter 47.
[13] Letter 35.
[14] Letter 24.
[15] Ibid.

his generous-flowing blood".[16] Jordan recalls unceasingly that the center of Dominican life is Jesus Christ, who restores all things in himself, in whom God has restored all things: the abbreviated Word—*Verbum abbreviatum*—a well-known patristic and medieval theme, but one which takes on a special resonance when used by a Friar Preacher and a "Sister Preacheress". With a touch of mischief, not having time to send the lengthy and edifying letter nuns like to receive, Jordan quite simply sends them Christ: "Word of salvation and grace, Word of sweetness and glory ... this is the Word upon which you must meditate, which you must turn over in your thoughts without ceasing. May he abide in you and live in you."[17]

The profound friendship, the community bonds between the brethren, sisters, and laity of the Order of Preachers have always existed. Since our era is more sensitive to this and talks more about it, seeing in it with good reason a paradigm of the "People of God", may this care for Dominican communion, may these bonds of the Dominican family, take inspiration above all from this return to the essential, which is preaching—in all its various modalities, and in harmony with various states of life and charisms—the Word of God.

In light of this we understand the amazing expression of Jordan to Diana: "Enter into the joy of

[16]Letter 45.
[17]Letter 31.

your Master." But he makes his meaning very clear:
"Your Master, that is, the Order of Preachers. Pray for
me and for the whole Order."[18]

---

[18] Letter 11.

FROM THE OFFICE OF READINGS
FOR THE MEMORIAL OF
BLESSED JORDAN OF SAXONY, PRIEST
FEBRUARY 13

A reading from the *Libellus on the Origins of the Order of Preachers* by blessed Jordan of Saxony, priest and second Master of the Order (Nn. 69, 75, 86–88, 110, 120: MOPH 16, Rome, 1935, pp. 57, 60, 66–67, 77, 81)

Putting off the Old Man, We Put on the New

When Brother Reginald, of happy memory, came to Paris and began his forceful preaching, I was moved by divine grace to conceive a desire to join his Order, and I made a promise to this effect in my mind, thinking that I had found precisely the safe path to salvation of a sort I had often thought about, even before I knew the brethren. Once my heart was confirmed, I began with all eagerness to try to entice my friend and companion to join me in my vow, seeing that he, both in his nature and his gifts of grace, would be a very useful preacher. He resisted, but, far from giving up, I did not abandon my efforts to persuade him.

When the day came on which, by the imposition of ashes, the faithful are reminded of their creation from the dust and their return to dust, we decided that it was a suitable occasion for us to begin our penance and to fulfill what we had vowed to the Lord. Our companions who lived in the same hospice with us were still unaware of our plans. When Brother Henry was leaving the hospice, one of them asked him, "Where are you going, Henry?" He answered, "I am going to Bethany." The student did not understand this saying, but the facts later made it clear to him when he saw Brother Henry entering Bethany, that is, "the house of obedience". The three of us went to St. Jacques, and we arrived in their midst, unexpectedly but opportunely, while the brethren were singing the antiphon *Immutemur habitu* ("Let us change our garments"). Without delay we put off the old man and put on the new, so that what they were singing with their voices was actually fulfilled in our deeds.

In the year of the Lord 1220, the first General Chapter of the Order was held in Bologna; I was present there myself, sent from Paris with three brethren, because Master Dominic had ordered us by letter to send four friars from the house in Paris to Bologna. But I had not yet completed two months in the Order at this time. At that same Chapter it was decreed, by the common consent of the brethren, that the General Chapter should be held one year in Bologna and the next in Paris, except that the following Chapter, in the following year, was to be held in Bologna. The same Chapter decreed that our brethren should thereafter no longer hold properties or revenues and that they should give up those that they already held in the district around Toulouse.

In the year of the Lord 1221, at the General Chapter in Bologna, they saw fit to make me the first provincial of the province of Lombardy, although I had only spent one year in the Order and had not struck root as deeply as I ought to have done. I was to be placed over others as their superior before I had learned to govern my own imperfection. At the same Chapter a community of friars was sent to England with Brother Gilbert as their prior. I was not present at this Chapter myself.

After the death of Master Dominic, there was a certain Brother Bernard of Bologna, who was plagued by a savage demon, so much so that he was driven day and night by horrible seizures of madness, which caused no end of disturbance to the company of the brethren. No doubt God's merciful providence had sent them this trial to exercise his servants' patience.

The fierce vexation of the above-mentioned Brother Bernard was the first occasion that prompted us to decide to sing the *Salve Regina* after Compline in Bologna. This practice spread from there to the rest of the province of Lombardy, and finally the same devout and healthful practice was adopted throughout the whole Order. A dependable religious once told me that he had often seen the mother of our Saviour in spirit; while the brethren were singing, "Turn then, most gracious advocate", the mother of our Lord was prostrating herself in the presence of her Son and praying for the safety of the whole Order. The memory of this ought to be preserved, so that when the brethren read of this, they will be inspired to even greater devotion in their praises of the Virgin.

℞. Christ sent me to preach the gospel, not with eloquent wisdom, lest the Cross of Christ be emptied of its power. * For the word of the Cross is folly to those who are perishing, but to us who are being saved, it is the power of God.

℣. For since, in the wisdom of God, the world did not know God through wisdom, it pleased God through the folly of what we preach to save those who believe. * For the word of the Cross is folly to those who are perishing, but to us who are being saved it is the power of God.

2

SAINT PETER OF VERONA:
THE BURDEN OF A HERITAGE

In every field of Western culture, any Dominican, especially the Dominican historian, runs into the ghosts of his ancestors—the Inquisitors. Their portraits hang in museums. In the Prado, in Madrid, Pedro Berruguete (+ 1504) presents a scene of trial by fire in which a haloed St. Dominic sits upon a high platform, presiding over a tribunal of the Inquisition. These ghosts have made their way into books. Who can forget the legend of the Grand Inquisitor that Ivan Karamazov tells to his brother Alyosha? This was a character probably inspired by the famous Spanish Dominican Inquisitor Thomas Torquemada (+ 1498). These ghosts still haunt stern architectural forms like the Holy Office in Rome, or the neighboring Santa Maria sopra Minerva not far from the Pantheon, or their like in Naples, Mexico City, and elsewhere. We even meet these specters in films such as *The Name of the Rose*, Umberto Eco's best-seller adapted for screen.

We observe there the confrontation between the meekness of a Franciscan nominalist and the severity bordering on fanaticism of a Dominican, Bernard Gui, played with melodramatic talent.

Though the Inquisitors included secular priests, Norbertines, Franciscans, and members of other Orders, the image that endures in the public imagination, whether we like it or not, is that of the black-and-white habit of the Friars Preachers. It is as if, by some contradiction, the black cappa and white tunic reveal something of the very Albigensian Manicheism we were fain to counteract.

We should not forget that Peter of Verona, called Peter Martyr (+ 1552), the first saint of the Order, after its Founder, to be canonized, was an Inquisitor. Born of Catharist parents, he entered the Dominican Order in 1221, a few months before the death of St. Dominic, who himself received him at Bologna. Pope Gregory IX named him Inquisitor for northern Italy, where there were still Manicheans. He preached to them with considerable success, if we accept the testimony of his biographer, Thomas Agni of Lentino. Traveling from Como to Milan with a companion, he was attacked by two assassins and suffered a hatchet blow to the head. The Tradition affirms that, dipping his finger in his own blood, he wrote on the ground *Credo in Deum*, then, after forgiving his murderer, died from a second blow.

In the following year he was canonized, after an inquiry in which the Holy See took an active part, an unusual intervention for that period. Some indications of protest against his elevation to the altar are extant in the contemporary documents of the Inquisition. Yet, by contrast, a very rich iconography of St. Peter Martyr developed. Easily recognizable is his head pierced from the hatchet blow, one finger to his lips, suggesting silence—somewhat paradoxical for one of the most venerated saints of an Order dedicated to the word—and in which the Inquisition was rightly conceived as an outgrowth of preaching. The iconography clearly makes the point that the word itself is born from meditative silence and explains why the image is so often found in Dominican refectories, where sacred and edifying texts are read aloud at silent meals. But above all its message communicates his destiny achieved in martyrdom's mute sacrifice. Fra Angelico, by placing Peter alongside St. Lawrence and his grill, holding a goose quill and the book of Scriptures, understood how to interpret him. Peter Martyr is so frequently represented in religious art because the Inquisitors adopted him as their patron saint and encouraged devotion to him through confraternities in his honor—an indication that the Order in no wise refused the inquisitorial burden and seemed to glory in being in the vanguard of the defense of the Catholic Faith.

In the nineteenth century, during the period of the July Monarchy in 1830, Lacordaire, the talented lawyer become secular priest, took notice of the Order of Preachers, which had been suppressed in France

since the French Revolution, and resolved to rees-
tablish it. Since he would have had to circumvent
laws still in force against religious congregations and
lacked the power to convince the government, he
decided, as a good orator and precursor of modern
means of communication, to address public opinion
directly. But Dominicans, being the Order of the
Inquisition, had the worst possible press. In 1814 Fer-
dinand VII had reintroduced the Spanish Inquisition
suppressed by Joseph Bonaparte. Its definitive suppres-
sion was as recent as 1820. In 1818 Antonio Llorente,
former secretary of the Inquisition in Madrid, published a book in French followed by one in Spanish,
which greatly contributed to the "black legend". This
legend could only stir up public opposition to Lacordaire, even though he was accurately considered to
hold liberal political ideas and to be daring in his prop-
ositions of separation of church and state.

In his "Memoir for the Reestablishment of the
Orders of Friars Preachers in France", published
in 1839, Lacordaire confronted the problem of the
Inquisition squarely, devoting to it his entire sixth
chapter. His weapons were successively defensive,
then offensive, his method historical, then journalistic.
He proposed to study "the past which is so liable to
misinterpretation" and then to study the present. The
former lawyer, the preacher of apologetics at Notre
Dame de Paris, took a kind of satisfaction in using
texts unfavorable a priori to his subject—such as a history of the Inquisition edited in Amsterdam in the late

seventeenth century by a Protestant and a "rational-istic and liberal" report of 1812 issued by the Span-ish Parliament, the Cortes. ("Monumental enemies", says Lacordaire.) Speaking always as a historian, in his self-description, bringing to the fore truths to unseat a misconception, Lacordaire wrote, "The Dominicans were neither the inventors, nor the promoters, nor the principal instruments of the Inquisition, and no one was less responsible than they for the Spanish excesses in this area. It is true, without a doubt, that they took part in the Inquisition, but who in Europe did not take part in it?"[1] He then moved to the attack, show-ing that concurrently in the 1830s there were Catho-lics being "persecuted" in Holland, Ireland, Poland, and Prussia. In a spirit of magnanimity, he concluded, "Let us be generous; let us concede, if you will, that truth and error were equally intolerant. Very well! What profit did the world gain from the deadly strug-gle? Truth did not destroy error, and error did not destroy truth."

His procedure therefore consisted in delimiting, the better to define, the institution of the Inquisition, setting it in its historical context, then clearing the reputation of the Order of Preachers as far as possi-ble, recognizing its participation in the Inquisition but insisting on the error in perspective that leads to intoler-ance. Not everyone was pleased with this presentation, and Dom Prosper Guéranger, who had enthusiastically

[1] *Oeuvres*, vol. 9 (Paris, 1911), p. 188.

encouraged Lacordaire to restore the Dominicans in France as he himself was doing with the Benedictines at Solesmes, reacted with vehemence and a certain harshness in correspondence that was, granted, private: "It is historically untrue that the Dominicans were not the men of the Inquisition within the Church.... It is very inappropriate to adopt the Order of Dominicans and reject one of its glories. If you do not understand the Holy Office, do not talk about being a Dominican. Moreover, if you ignore history, do not write nineteenth-century history."[2] Accused by Guéranger of scorning this "honor" enjoyed by the Dominicans of being this Order of the Inquisition (cf. *Année liturgique*, precisely on the feastday of St. Peter of Verona), Lacordaire replied, "Your understanding of the Dominican spirit appears to me radically false, and in any case mine is quite different: I see it as the only true, the only useful, the only Christian spirit."[3]

The controversy is past history, but all the same it poses the question of the Inquisition in terms of a heritage. In the Dominican Order, diversified as it is, it is a matter not of either claiming or refusing this heritage but rather of knowing how to take responsibility for it. It seems to me that in the interests of consistency, no heritage can be accepted without a certain evaluation that true historians have, over a period of time, been able to make.

[2] Letter of May 12, 1839, to Madame Swetchine.
[3] Letter of August 10, 1839.

Without playing Lacordaire's role, I may be allowed
to say that to attribute to St. Dominic the function
of Inquisitor has no foundation, and this for a purely
chronological reason: he died at Bologna in 1221,
and the special tribunals of the Inquisition were not
set up until 1231, in Lombardy and Germany, by the
common decision of the Pope and Emperor. Michelet
was obviously biased when he wrote in his *Histoire
de France*, "This Dominic, awesome founder of the
Inquisition, was a noble Castilian. No one surpassed
him for the gift of tears, a characteristic often found in
conjunction with fanaticism."[4] Moreover, St. Dominic's well-known and moving compassion, witnessed
to in his process of canonization and the earliest biographies, a trait that was considered his chief characteristic, kept him far from the Albigensian Crusade.
When the King of France sent Simon de Montfort
and his barons from the north to oppose the Catharist heresy in battle, after the numerous and fruit-
less preaching campaigns, I imagine that Dominic, so
concerned for the Catholic Faith, might lend approval
to this appeal to force but would have nothing to do
with it himself. His first biography—about which we
can have no scruples—expressly says, "Brother Dominic kept to his role of tireless preacher of the word
of God."[5] The operative word is not "kept to" (*man-
sit*), which might be ambiguous, but "preacher", for

[4] II, bk. IV, chap. 7.
[5] *Libellus* 34.

it implies the dimension of mercy and exhortation, which is supported by the rest of the biographical text. Could St. Francis of Assisi ever be accused of intolerance? The same goes for his contemporary and friend St. Dominic.

Specialists in the history of common law have shown clearly a progression in the procedure of the Inquisition in regard to human rights, offering a suspected person juridical guarantees that most of the Inquisitors honored. But this in no way hindered imbalance in some who had access to this awe-inspiring power, such as the terrible Robert le Bougre in the north of France. At the same time, we must recognize that the process of the Inquisition led to certain excesses. Political, national, and probably also economic interests had a considerable part to play in a system of complete osmosis between church and state. This was the case in the trial of Joan of Arc. We should also distinguish carefully between the Inquisition of the medieval type, at the service of the bishops and then of the papacy, and the Spanish Inquisition. Founded in 1478, this latter followed the ancient rules of procedure and juridical protection of the former institution but differed widely from it, becoming actually an instrument in the hands of the Spanish monarchy, which named the Inquisitor General. Furthermore, in the modern period, for ecclesiological and political reasons, the Inquisition in France and England was only nominal.

Thus the basic problem posed by the Inquisition is that of coercion in spiritual matters. The institution of the Inquisition belongs to a system of defense of a society, Western Christianity, which welds together the Catholic Church and temporal society for the purpose of making faith and Christianity the foundation of the social order.

It was in the name of duty that sovereigns intervened to defend the Faith. To rebel against the Catholic Faith (and the Protestant faith also, after the sixteenth century) was to rebel against the prince. In the midst of the anxiety concerning salvation prevalent at the time, the people, in the Church's estimation, needed this kind of protection against the spread of doctrine that precipitated eternal damnation. Against dissenters, preventive measures and therapeutic action were considered necessary. Against the stubborn, excision of the diseased from the Body of Christ, turning them over to the secular authority in charge of public welfare, was perceived as warranted.

The great Erasmus, returning to the sources, those of the gospel and the Fathers of the Church, was one of the first to perceive the profound contradiction of what was later to be called religious intolerance. He categorically criticized the practices of the Spanish monks.[6] This Christian humanist, an enemy to clamor and war, believed that the Church ought to follow the example of her Founder, who did not break the

[6] *Adversus monachos quidam hispanos*, Title IV: *Contra sanctam haereticorum inquisitionem*, objection 22, *Opera omnia*, Leiden, vol. IX, 1054D–1055D).

bruised reed or quench the smoldering wick.[7] After the example of his master, Augustine, he pondered on the darnel mixed with the good wheat until the end of the world, when the harvester should come.

Confronted with this Dominican heritage, should we make honorable amends? I believe this is not really the problem. Rather, the problem is twofold, historical and theological. The historian should beware at all costs of falling into his pet sin, unforgivable nevertheless: anachronism. He may not assess an institution if he is ignorant of its values. The best he can do is to pore over the texts and study mentalities with that empathy that is indispensable for understanding. Then he will see that the swift canonization of St. Peter of Verona crowned first his zeal for the Faith and above all his martyrdom, even if the image of the saint has become a banner or emblem of a system that he must judge theologically (or philosophically or even what we might call ideologically).

Thinking of Catholic theologians, it seems to me that a proper assessment of religious liberty was given by Cardinal Journet in a brief intervention during the last session of Vatican II, September 21, 1965. In substance, the aged Cardinal whom Paul VI admired so deeply showed that society and the Church, influenced by mature reflection coming from different positions and from the preaching of the gospel, had reached a more penetrating and nuanced understanding of man.

[7] Is 42:1–4; Mt 12:18–20.

To the famous phrase still advanced by many Catholics that "truth alone has rights" should be joined, the Cardinal declared, the phrase "but the person, each person, has even more fundamental rights". He added that we have progressively reached a more explicit distinction between the temporal and the spiritual. This is why the Church continues to oppose error, "but with the weapons of light, not the weapons of war".

In the past, Dominicans were named *pugiles fidei* (champions of the Faith). Quiet reflection upon our forebears of the Inquisition should persuade us to gird ourselves now with the weapons of light, which bear such names as humble and patient pursuit of truth, dialogue, and tolerance, first clothing ourselves, no less, with the confession of faith, the affirmation of hope, and the stamina of unfailing charity!

A reading from a letter of Roderic of Atencia to Saint Raymond of Peñafort, priest and third Master of the Order (*Année dominicaine ou Vie des saints, bienheureux, martyrs* O.P., vol. 4, Lyons, 1889, pp. 901–3)

He Presented His Life and the Praises of the Paschal Victim as an Offering

It happened that Brother Peter decided, for the cause of the Faith, to take the road from Como to Milan on the Sunday after Easter, the same route he had taken the previous sabbath. After he had received a blessing early that morning, and as he was thinking about starting his journey, it suddenly entered his heart to celebrate the Mass of the Resurrection. He prostrated himself at the feet of a brother who was to go with him and confessed with more than his customary care and attention (as that brother reported in his own account). He celebrated Mass with devotion and then set out with three of the brethren. As those brothers later recalled, while they were traveling he spoke with great devotion only about the bravest sufferings of some of the martyrs. When he had finished the lengthy discourse, he began to sing with a loud voice (which was not his custom) the sequence *Victimae paschali laudes* and immediately ordered Brother

Dominic (who was to become a companion in his coming suffering) to join in. When another one of the brethren, Conrad by name, began to sing in harmony, Brother Peter kindly turned to him and said, "Please, allow me to sing this alone, along with Brother Dominic, for you are not singing together with us." So these two brothers, with the other brother silent, sang the whole sequence in a loud voice.

When they had finished, they came to a certain town in the diocese of Milan called Meda, about lunchtime. In order to avoid burdening any one host, they split up for lunch: two went to one place, while Brother Peter with Brother Dominic turned off to a certain monastery, where they found lunch prepared. They ate quickly and sent word to the other brothers that they were leaving and that the others should follow when they had finished their own lunch. Peter resumed his journey, hastening toward his crown.

When they came to a little hill about two miles from the village, two hired mercenaries, ministers of Satan, lay concealed. They had seen the brethren coming from far away and made plans for their murder; but one of them, stricken with a sense of repentance, was afraid to consent to this crime and, running away from the other, hurried to the nearby town with swift strides. There he found the other two brethren, and with tears he told them about the whole wicked plan. The other brothers then began to run with all their might to save Brother Peter; but when they arrived at the place, they found that the other minister of Satan had murdered Brother Peter most cruelly with five blows of the sickle.

When Peter was struck, as his companion (who survived for another six days) has testified, Peter followed the example of the Savior. He did not murmur, he did not defend himself nor flee, but generously bore the blows with courage. He prayed for his murderer with hands raised toward heaven in a clear voice, saying, "Into your hands, O Lord, I commend my spirit." He handed over his undefiled spirit to Christ, who died and rose again, at about the time of None, at the sixth hour.

Responsory   Cf. Jn 1:20; Eph 5:2

℟. I fully rejoice that I have been counted worthy to become a sacrifice for Christ: when accused, I did not deny his holy name, but confessed him to be the Christ. * When struck, I gave thanks (*T.P.* alleluia).

℣. I made myself a sacrifice to God with a fragrant offering. * When struck, I gave thanks (*T.P.* alleluia).

3

SAINT THOMAS AQUINAS
AND THE SEARCH FOR TRUTH

WITH THE POSSIBLE EXCEPTIONS of St. Augustine and Shakespeare, there is no other writer
whose work has been commented on, compared to
other thinkers, and subjected to criticism more than
that of St. Thomas Aquinas. And no other author has
been exalted higher than the Angelic Doctor. No other
has been declared common Doctor of the Church, as
Pope Pius XI did, resurrecting a title accorded Thomas
in the fourteenth century! His philosophy is taken for
granted as *perennial*, and his theology merits the same
tribute. After all the panegyrics—fewer nowadays
doubtless in faculties of theology, lessening even as his
actual feast-day, March 7, the anniversary of his death,
has been transferred to January 28, the date of the
transferral of his body to Toulouse in 1369—after so
many feast-day sermons, so many scientific or edifying
biographies (not necessarily incompatible), what is left
for me to say, and that in a brief space? It is always

possible to return to the sources of our knowledge of St. Thomas the person—that is, not so much to his works, which contain no personal references save for the few rare allusions that have given rise to some conjectures, but rather to his earliest biography. I shall gladly limit myself to this.

The first biography was drawn up in view of his canonization by Brother William of Tocco, prior of Benevento, to be used at the inquiry about St. Thomas' miracles, held in 1317. It is true that modern historians have contested many of the facts reported, and particularly William's chronology. This is why it is a good idea to consult simultaneously the most recent and complete of Thomas' biographies, that of James A. Weisheipl, *Friar Thomas d'Aquino, His Life, Thought and Works.*[1]

But Tocco interests me because he gives a spiritual and ingenuous view of the profound vocation of Thomas Aquinas, the view held by the Order forty years after his death and one that it wished to communicate to the Church. The latter would, after the doctrinal disputes linked with St. Thomas' name in Paris, declare his sanctity. I am interested here less in the list of his works or great theses than in the form of his spiritual genius, the signs that reveal a temperament, a stance before God.

It is true that many things in Tocco's account make us smile, especially when he tries to discover

[1] Washington, 1974, 1983.

in Thomas' childhood unquestionable grounds for his theological vocation. If baby Thomas "began to cry, refusing to be consoled by the caresses of his nurse, only a scrap of parchment with writing on it could succeed in quenching his tears".[2] Even granted that this may have happened, we should now hesitate to see in the incident a foreshadowing of his rumination of the Scriptures or a reference to the eating of the little scroll in the book of Revelation!

But what is remarkable is the insistence with which Tocco wishes to show how Thomas gave himself wholly to the search for truth. It seems that it was less a proclamation of the truth, a confession of faith, than an arduous, difficult, sometimes exhausting search for this truth, a life inseparable from study and prayer. This was demanding work: from the Scriptures theologians "extracted the kernel of a difficult text".[3] And throughout his account of his life, miracles, and visions, Tocco reveals to us Thomas' genial and wholly simple personality.

A Man of Overwhelming Honesty

Nicholas, the Cistercian abbot of Fossanova where Thomas died on his way to the Second Council of Lyons, on being questioned in view of the canonization, gives a description so condensed as to border

[2] *Vita* 4.
[3] Chap. 1.

on understatement. "Brother Thomas was a man of great honesty of life, great purity, and great holiness. Every day, when in good health, he celebrated the Holy Sacrifice and passed his time in ceaseless study and prayer."[4]

The "dumb Ox", as his brethren nicknamed him, was notably taciturn and silent, "eager at study and given to prayer" (*in studio assiduus et in oratione devotus*).[5] All were struck by the humility of this extraordinary mind. Tocco has this to say: "He was aware that all his knowledge was God's gift; this is why no movement of vainglory could ever darken his soul, knowing as he did that each day he received the light of divine truth. His humble manner of life was an indication of his virtue; it reflected what transpired in his soul."[6] When a young disciple of a great master like St. Albert, he was cautious about revealing his fine memory[7] and the rapidity and subtlety of his reasoning at the very age when a man wants to stand out.

His attachment to the Dominican Order, which ran so counter to his family's wishes in the beginning, is itself a proof of his disinterestedness and his desire for humility. When Thomas was making his novitiate in Paris in 1245, thirty years after the foundation of the Dominicans, the Order of Preachers was hardly a good choice for a member of a Neapolitan family caught up

---

[4] Ferrua, *Thomae Aquinatis Vitae Fontes*, p. 214.
[5] Tocco, chap. 13.
[6] Chap. 25.
[7] Chap. 42.

in the struggles between Emperor and Pope. It offered no advantage from the point of view of social or political prestige. It opened no doors to money and power, and this was what frustrated his mother and brothers, who would have liked to make a Benedictine abbot of Monte Cassino out of him—there where he had spent his childhood!

Tocco also shows us how Thomas Aquinas lived a life of obedience. He was indeed an intellectual, but for the sake of the Church. He served her first of all by teaching. From the time of his ordination in 1250 he never ceased to travel, putting himself at the service of theology students in Paris, Naples, Orvieto, Rome, Paris again, and finally Naples. It was in obedience to the Pope that he set out for the Council of Lyons, which he never reached, but for which he had drawn up his treatise on "The Errors of the Greeks". He often served as an expert in the course of his life. His ability to mark off the frontiers of the temporal and spiritual (the *De regno*, doubtless destined for the King of Cyprus) is well known and also his defense of the mendicants against the secular attacks led by William of St. Amour. Yet a mere glance at the list of his works shows that many of them are answers to questions or consultations. Tocco tells us that King Saint Louis was accustomed to ask his advice: "When the King needed, on the following day, counsel on some difficult and urgent point, he would confide this to the Doctor on the previous evening, that he might concentrate on it during the night. Obedient as he was, Thomas acquiesced in this as if the request were a command."[8]

Speaking of St. Louis, we recall the well-known and amusing story of St. Thomas dining at the King's table, to show how his intellectual life continued uninterrupted, an essential part of Thomas wherever he might be. Having accepted the royal invitation out of obedience, he remained absorbed in his thoughts and suddenly struck the table, crying, "That's the end of the Manichean heresy!" He had found a clinching argument, so to speak. A painting of Nicholas Manuel Deutsch in the fifteenth century illustrates this incident. Brother Thomas, his head covered and with a halo, and the dove representing the Holy Spirit breathing into his ear, dictates the argument to a scribe summoned by the King, while the prior of St. Jacques pulls at his cappa "to make him come back from his abstraction to the world around him", as Tocco delightfully remarks.[9]

A Man of Desires

Thomas was, therefore, possessed by the search for wisdom. He sought it with his whole soul and all his powers. According to Tocco, it figured in his dreams, was present in his prayer. "When he encountered some difficulty before having had recourse to

[8] Chap. 36.
[9] Chap. 44.

prayer, he would set himself to pray and miraculously would find the solution to his problems."[10] William of Tocco, and also the depositions made at the process of canonization, emphasize the strong connection Thomas made between study and prayer. Peter Grasso of Naples says, "He was always either teaching, writing, dictating, praying, or preaching", while Brother James de Cajazzo declares, "He gave himself without respite to prayer, study, and writing."

He had the gift of going directly to the heart of the matter in his reading. Tocco comments, "Since divine providence had destined him to plumb the sacred mysteries, it was only fitting that the Spirit of God should hide nothing from this man of desires"—thus giving him the name attributed to the prophet Daniel in the Vulgate (Dan 10:5).[11]

The renowned phrase that has embodied the strategy of the Dominican Order—*contemplare et contemplata aliis tradere*—"to contemplate and to give to others the fruits of contemplation"[12]—corresponds perfectly to this intellectual ideal. It is symbolized by Jacob's ladder. Love of God and neighbor motivates transmission of the message contemplated. We must ascend and descend upon Jacob's ladder[13] like the angels, who while occupied with man never lose sight of God. The unity bonding the contemplative

[10] Chap. 31.

[11] Tocco, *Hystoria beati Thomae de Aquino*, chap. 40.

[12] S.T. IIa-IIae, q. 188, a. 6.

[13] Gen 28:12 and Jn 1:51.

life with the works of the active life such as teaching or preaching[14] is through love. And wisdom's love reminds us that human life reaches its zenith in the contemplative vision of trinitarian life.

We must also recall St. Thomas' devotion to the Eucharist and to Christ crucified. This is clearly shown in the well-known episode of his search for a solution to the objection "concerning eucharistic accidents without a subject" (*de accidentibus existentibus sine subjecto*). Having been asked to explain this in a "sententia", Thomas approached the altar and laid down his notebook containing the response he had drawn up. Then, "lifting his hands toward the crucifix, he prayed earnestly that he might teach according to the truth". We know the answer of Christ, who appeared standing before him: "You have written well concerning the Sacrament of my Body and my Blood."[15] This account is complemented by another passage[16] where Jesus asks him, "What reward will you have for your labor?" Thomas cries out in a burst of love, "Lord, I will have yourself! *Domine, non nisi te*!" We note that his manner of praying with uplifted arms recalls "St. Dominic's ways of prayer".

We are almost astonished by the role St. Thomas gives to reason and nature in his work. And yet, it is in this establishment of the relationship between faith and reason that we find his own decisive and unequaled

[14] IIa-IIae, q. 181, a. 3.
[15] Chap. 53.
[16] Chap. 35.

role in the history of Christian thought. Reason finds access to the truths of faith by way of analogies, which are neither demonstrations nor proofs of reason but paths leading to the highest truth given through revelation. We have to bear in mind the profound biblical comparison St. Thomas gives in answering the objection that by using reason, one waters down the strong wine of divine wisdom, the heady wine of the word of God. He answers simply, No! for as happened at the marriage in Cana, this water is turned into wine! This sainted theologian, who ranks among the most speculative of Christian thinkers, teaches us how devotion to the humanity of Christ is a pedagogue, one especially adapted to lead to divinity. "Christ's humanity is like a guide taking us by the hand", he says.[17]

If I had to say what was the most valuable contribution St. Thomas made to Christian thought, however, I would choose the saying that is perhaps the most quoted and that I think is the most essential: *Gratia non destruit naturam sed elevat et perficit*—Grace does not destroy nature but elevates and perfects it.[18] It seems to me that forgetting this central truth has been, in the history of Christianity, the source of all the imbalances between thought and action.

Presuming its authenticity, I would also add something St. Thomas himself articulated in a homily for the second Sunday of Advent, saying, "When

[17] Torrell, *Dictionnaire de Spiritualitée*, col. 746, citing IIa-IIae, q. 81, a. 3 ad 2.
[18] Ia-IIae, q. 1, a. 8 ad 2.

Aristotle was asked where he had learned so much, he answered, 'From created things which know not how to lie'." Moving from his use of this quotation, we discover in Thomas himself an optimism about creation that is Christian, springing from the very goodness of God. For Thomas applied himself to the study of the virtues, seeing them in no way threatening nature, which grace brings to perfection. Creation, in his understanding, contains its own proper and legitimate sphere of secondary causality. All of this taken together leads to an incomparable balance between nature and grace. Pope Paul VI expressed this perfectly in his letter on the seventh centenary of St. Thomas' death in 1974, saying that his genius "rests on a harmonization of the world's secularity with the radical demands of the gospel, thus avoiding the unnatural tendency to despise the world and its values while at the same time not betraying in any way the basic principles governing the supernatural order".[19]

The grandeur of Aquinas lies in this firmly rooted realism that finds its full breadth in the revelation of the immensity and gratuity of divine grace. The Angelic Doctor shows us how we must unite intense and necessary study with the joy of prayer. Appreciating St. Thomas' joining of mystical wisdom and theological wisdom, Cardinal Journet wrote tellingly, "Like some brother gardener of a contemplative monastery who, although his silent soul abounds in mystical graces, is

[19] *The Pope Speaks*, vol. 19, 1975, p. 292.

yet glad to yield for the common good to the hum-
blest of work, he observed with the greatest respect
and the gentlest patience the rules imposed on him by
the nature of the matter entrusted to his care."[20]

[20] *Introduction à la Théologie*; English trans., *The Wisdom of Faith*,
p. 13.

A reading from a lesser theological work (*On the Reasons of the Faith*) of Saint Thomas Aquinas, priest and Doctor of the Church (*De rationibus fidei*, Leonine ed., vol. 40, Rome, 1969, pp. 56ff.)

The Foolishness of God Is Wiser Than Men

Christ chose to have poor parents, who nevertheless were perfect in virtue, lest anyone should glory in nobility of birth or family wealth alone. He lived a poor life to teach us to despise riches. He lived an ordinary life without the trappings of dignity to call men back from an inordinate desire for honors. He endured labor, hunger, thirst, and bodily beating so that those intent on pleasure and extravagance might be drawn back to the good of virtue by the harshness of this life.

Finally he suffered death, lest anyone neglect truth on account of the fear of death. Lest anyone dread a vile death on behalf of the truth, he chose the meanest kind of death, namely, death on a cross. And so it was fitting that the Son of God, who had been made man, should suffer death, that by his example he might encourage men to virtue. Thus what Peter says is true: *Christ suffered for us, leaving us an example, that we might follow in his footsteps.*

For if he had lived as a rich man in the world, as a powerful man or surrounded by some sort of great dignity, it would be possible to believe that he had received his teaching and miracles by the favor of men and human power. Therefore, so that it might be evident as a work of divine power, he chose everything that was base and weak in the world: a poor mother, a needy life, unlearned disciples and messengers, to be rebuked and condemned by the powerful of the world even to death, so that it would appear quite clearly that the source of his miracles and teaching was not human power but divine.

Concerning this point we must consider that it was according to the same reason of providence by which the Son of God, having become man, willed to suffer weakness. He even chose his disciples, those ministers of human salvation, and wished them to be abased in the world: he chose not lettered and noble men but ignorant and lowly men, poor men—even fishermen. Sending them out to procure the salvation of men, he ordered them to preserve poverty, to suffer persecutions and insult, and even to undergo death for the truth, lest their preaching seem designed for some earthly comfort and that the salvation of the world be ascribed not to earthly wisdom or strength but only to divine. Therefore divine power, working miraculous deeds, was not lacking in those who, according to the world, seemed to be of no account.

This was necessary for human restoration, that men might learn to place their trust not in themselves,

proudly, but in God. This was necessary for the perfection of human righteousness, so that man might
subject himself completely to God, from whom he
hopes to receive all good things that are to come, and
to recognize those that he has already received.

Responsory   2 Tim 4:8; 1:12

℟. The crown of righteousness is set aside for me,
which the Lord will give me * as a just judge on
that day.

℣. I know the one in whom I have believed, and I
am convinced that he is able to preserve what I have
entrusted to him * as a just judge on that day.

4

SAINT CATHERINE OF SIENA
AND LOVE FOR THE CHURCH

S T. CATHERINE OF SIENA'S ENTIRE LIFE, we can affirm, is marked by love for the Church. We find the strongest affirmation of this in the *Dialogue* and in the numerous authentic letters that have come down to us. We find it in an extended way in the biography that I shall use here, the *Legenda Major*, written by Blessed Raymond of Capua, her spiritual director, and later abridged by another confessor, Thomas Caffarini.

Born in 1347, a year before the advent of the Black Plague, which devastated the West, Catherine Benincasa experienced her first vision at the age of six, a vision already ecclesially oriented. Over the church of the Friars Preachers in Siena she saw Christ vested in pontifical robes and wearing the papal tiara, surrounded by the Apostles Peter, Paul, and John. He silently blessed her.

After receiving at the age of eighteen the black-and-white habit of the Sisters of Penance of St.

Dominic, "the white symbolizing innocence and the black humility", this mantellata was led to marriage "in faith" with Christ. In a vision known to mysticism within the Church and elsewhere in the Order, Christ exchanged his heart with his servant Catherine.

The Lord asked her to remain in the world and to practice the works of mercy there: "I will be your guide in all that you have to do."[1] It was at this time that, noted for miracles and mystical prodigies, which Raymond recounts in detail, she began to attract a host of people and to gather around her the most fervent of them, her *family*, her *bella brigata*—her *beautiful band*.

In 1370 came an encounter decisive for her but still more for Raymond. Catherine then busied herself with getting the Pope to return from his "captivity" in Avignon, and 1376 witnessed her famous sojourn in Avignon with Gregory XI, crowned with success even though not due solely to Catherine.[2]

In 1377 Catherine retired to Rocca d'Orcia, where she had her vision of the *Dialogue*, which she then dictated and which was completed in October of 1378 (referred to in the *Legend* as the "Book"). But at this moment the Church was being devastated by another plague: schism. Two claimants contended for the Chair of Peter. Rallying without hesitation to the support of the Italian Pope residing in Rome, Urban VI,

---

[1] *Legend* II, 1, 121–22.
[2] *Legend* II, 10, 289.

Catherine was to live out the last months of her life in the grief of seeing the garment of Christ torn and in ardent supplication for the cessation of the scandal. In 1380 she had one last great vision of the Bark of Peter and died on April 29 at the age of thirty-three, a symbolic number that has been contested along with other points in Raymond's *Life*.

On the preceding Pentecost, at Bologna, her disciple and spiritual heir, Raymond of Capua, had just been elected Master of the Order of Preachers. He was to attempt, with some measure of success, to carry out the intuitions of the Siennese saint in reforming the Dominicans.

To Love the Church Is to Long for Her Renewal

The idea of reform, of renewal, is fundamental in Catherine's vision of the Church. The Church of Christ should renew herself in each epoch, not in her divine structure but in her members,[3] putting on the new man of which St. Paul speaks. The reform must begin with the head, and prelates should act "according to justice, humility, burning charity, and the light of discretion".[4] They should beware lest the other members of the Church perish, "rooting up the briars of sin". The example of religious Orders is basic, and that is why they should cleanse themselves and

[3] Letter 346 to Urban VI.
[4] *Dialogue* 119.

work for the eradication of the most terrible evils of
the time: schism and heresy.

In the *Dialogue* Catherine asks God to reform his
Church,[5] and the Lord responds with a promise of
mercy in answer to the prayer of saints. "With these
prayers, sweat and tears, I shall wash the face of my
spouse, holy Church, for I have already shown her
to you with the features of a woman so befouled as to
resemble a leper. It is the fault of my ministers, and
of all those Christians who indulge themselves in the
heart of this spouse." This promise is then made solemnly to Catherine by God, "for the mystical Body
of the Church", according to the expression used in
Chapter 86 of the *Dialogue*. It is here that one can
speak of that "experiential knowledge by virtue of
which an individual soul can suffer in a marvelous way
the universal mystery of the Church", of which Cardinal Journet speaks at the beginning of his great work,
The Church of the Word Incarnate, placing it under the
patronage of St. Catherine of Siena.

The Apostolate of Prayer

With the wisdom springing from her experience of
holiness, Catherine set herself to pray for the Church
with all her strength: "I implore you to fulfill what
you are causing me to ask you"[6] "through the fruit

[5] Chap. 13.
[6] *Dialogue*, chap. 134.

of your Son's blood". Catherine offered her life for the Church.[7] In her letters to the great personages of the Church, she shows this zeal for the healing of the Church through her purification. Thus we read her simple advice to the Cardinal of Ostia:[8] "I wish you to be occupied with nothing but loving God, saving souls, and serving the sweet spouse of Christ." She exhorts him, as she does so many others, to "act manfully", courageously: "If he has to lay down his life, do it!"

In her legacy to Raymond of Capua,[9] she recounts how in Rome, during Lent of 1380, "truly dead", for she was "without any nourishment", she was transported, from the time the bell rang for Matins until the end of Mass, to the Basilica of St. Peter. "I went in, and I set to work immediately for the Bark of Holy Church. I remained there until evening, and I did not wish to leave this place all day and all night." "To work"—that is, obviously, to pray for the Church and "the bark of Holy Church", a traditional image but doubtless evoked by the Ship represented in a mosaic of Giotto that could be seen at that time in St. Peter's in Rome. Catherine's mission focused on the needs of the Church and of Christianity. She had Masses celebrated "exclusively for the intention of Holy Church".

Two months later, on the Sunday before the Ascension, Catherine entered into her agony. According to

[7] Prayer XI to the Virgin and XXVI to the Father.
[8] Letter 11.
[9] I, 373.

the account left us by Barduccio Canigiani, she prayed at length in these words, audacious, actually, which show her absolute love for the Church: "Merciful Father, you have always urged me to struggle with you for the salvation of the world and the reform of Holy Church, with my sweet, loving, grieving desires, with my tears and humble, continual, and faithful prayer—but I have slept in the bed of negligence. This is why so many evils and ruins have befallen your Church." Catherine's holiness consisted not in seeing the misfortunes of the Church and pointing out who was responsible for them but rather in attributing to herself the effects of sin in the Church. She could not separate herself from sinners in the Church but was herself one of them and thought she had been nothing but a "mirror of misery" to the countless souls God had entrusted to her. Pious exaggeration? On the contrary, a sense of the unworthiness of one who was not, before the One who is, according to the expression that is not only frequent in her writings but also essential to her theology.[10]

Catherine, Doctor of the Church

The whole *Dialogue* is based, as we know, on four great pleas: for herself, for one cannot truly help one's neighbor unless one first helps oneself; for the reform of the Church; for the world, and peace among

[10] *Legend*, I, 10; II, 1, 121.

Christians, and the metaphor of Christ the Bridge between God and men corresponds to this; and finally a particular intention, the mission of Raymond of Capua. We can see from this that Catherine's prayer is both universal and limited, general and particular.

St. Catherine's teaching on prayer forms part of her instruction as a Doctor of the Church. We find it dispersed throughout all her work, but particularly in the *Dialogue*, whose final chapter is itself a wonderful hymn to the Trinity. We find it also in a letter addressed to her niece, Sister Eugenia, a nun at Montepulciano, where she briefly summarizes the threefold way of prayer. First, there is the prayer of the heart, namely, continual prayer, or that constant and holy desire that keeps one in the presence of God. By this form of prayer, Catherine takes up an important teaching of St. Augustine, who remarked that, first of all, one's prayer is one's desire. Secondly, there is vocal prayer, especially that of the Divine Office, wherein our heart must be in accord with our tongue. Thirdly, there is mental prayer, in which the soul "unites itself to God in a movement of love. Rising above itself through the light of its intelligence, it sees; it knows and clothes itself in truth."

In describing Catherine's prayer, Raymond of Capua followed the qualities that Aquinas presents in his *Summa Theologiae*.[11] But we can make explicit what Raymond implied in his biography,[12] namely,

[11] IIa-IIae, q. 183, a. 15.
[12] I, 3, 38.

that her prayer was truly apostolic, ecclesial, and by consequence very Dominican. Can we not say that like the Church, prayer itself is "a mother"? It nourishes, it teaches, it protects, it guides. As the Eternal Father revealed to Catherine, prayer is an apostolic mission. In "the cell of self-knowledge", he said to her, "it is through your tears, through your humble and constant prayer, that I wish to show my mercy to the world." In this compassionate love, Catherine of Siena is truly the daughter of St. Dominic.

From a letter to the novices of the Order of Saint
Mary of the Mount of Olives from Saint Catherine
of Siena, virgin and Doctor of the Church (*Ep.* 36:
ed. P. Misciattelli, vol. I, Florence, 1970, pp. 136–42)

You Shall Find a Spring of Charity in the Side of the Crucified Christ

My dearest children in Jesus Christ:

I, Catherine, servant and slave of the servants of
Jesus Christ, write to you in his precious blood, wish-
ing to see you children obedient unto death, learning from the spotless Lamb who was obedient to his
Father, even to the horrible death of the Cross.

Mark well how he is the way and the rule, which
both you and all other creatures ought to follow. I
would like you to place him always before your
mind's eye. Look at how obedient this Word is! He
did not refuse any work that he had received from his
Father because of its heaviness, but on the contrary,
he ran forward with the greatest desire. This was most
evident at the Last Supper, when he said, "With desire
I have desired to eat this Passover with you, before I
die." *To eat this Passover* is the same as to fulfill the will
of the Father and the desire of the Son. Since he saw

that he had very little time left (for he saw that he was about to offer the ultimate sacrifice to the Father on our behalf), he rejoiced and was glad and said with joy, "With desire I have desired this."

And this was the Passover of which he spoke: to give himself as food and to offer the sacrifice of his own body in obedience to his Father. Jesus had eaten the Passover on other occasions with his disciples, but never in the same way as he did now. O love beyond all telling, most sweet and most burning! You are not thinking about the torment at all, nor about your shameful death. The Word sees that he was chosen by the Father and took humanity as a spouse. He was ordered to shed his blood for us so that the will of God might be fulfilled in us, that we might be sanctified in his blood.

So, I pray you, my sweet children in sweet Christ Jesus, never be afraid of anything but always rely on the blood of Christ crucified. Do not separate yourselves from him in temptations and error; you can neither persevere with fear, nor can you maintain obedience and the Order with dread.

Therefore I never want you to fear: let all servile fear be taken away from you. With sweet Paul may you say lovingly, "Be strong today, my soul. *I can do all things through Christ* crucified; he who comforts me is within me in love and desire." Love, love, love! The one who is in the world finds that the sea crashed upon his ship, but whoever is in holy religion sails in the vessel of another, that is, of the Order.

Take courage! You will find the spring of charity in the side of the crucified Christ. I want you to make ready your place and your house. Rise up with great and burning desire; hurry, enter, and stay in this sweet house. Neither demons nor any other creature can take this away from you or stop you from reaching your final goal, which is *the knowledge and love of God.* I shall not say any more: abide in the holy and sweet love of God. Love, love one another.

Responsory

℟. Nothing seemed more satisfying to this Virgin, nothing more worthy in all creation, than the commands of Jesus Christ * and to lead everyone to eternal life.

℣. She committed herself to the task of calling back the lost * and to lead everyone to eternal life.

5

FRA ANGELICO:
PREACHING THROUGH BEAUTY

O<small>N OCTOBER</small> 3, 1982, Pope John Paul II, in an apostolic letter issued "by his own authority", granted to the entire Order of Preachers the liturgical cult of Fra John of Fiesole under the title of "Blessed". This was the ratification of a long Tradition, which poses a primary question: Does Fra Angelico merit the title of "Blessed" because of the beauty of his religious art or, instead, because he was a holy man who was able to create paintings that penetrate so deeply into theological mystery? The Pope partially answers this question by quoting from the classic biography of Fra Angelico written by Giorgio Vasari a century after the death of the Dominican of Fiesole: "His painting was the fruit of the great harmony between a holy life and the creative power with which he had been endowed."

Let us recall some of the elements of his life, divided between the Dominican cloister and the various commissions given him, those paintings that now leave traces of light in museums. If we adopt the traditional dating, Guido di Piero (to use his baptismal name) was born around 1400 in the valley of Mugello in Tuscany. His earliest works go back to the years 1415–17, and his name is found in the roster of a "guild" attached to a church in Florence: he was entered there by a renowned painter of miniatures. At that time he frequented the Dominican convent of Santa Maria Novella, which was a center of the reform of religious life inspired by Blessed John Dominic (1357–1419), himself a disciple of St. Catherine of Siena. The Western Schism had just ended. The conventual church had been consecrated in the presence of the new Roman Pope, Martin V, in 1420.

It was around this time that Guido entered the Order of Preachers at San Domenico in Fiesole: its prior was soon to be Brother Antoninus Pierozzi, the future holy archbishop of Florence, who at the time was vicar general of the reformed houses. Brother John was ordained to the priesthood in 1427 or 1428. Numerous works of his executed for churches or convents in Florence and Fiesole belong to this period; laconic documents allow us to date them, signatures, for example, or notations on registers or receipts. Brother John remained assigned at Fiesole, where he fulfilled various conventual duties.

The Friars Preachers took possession of the church and convent of St. Mark in Florence in 1436. They soon began to restore it and then to enlarge it by building a dormitory. Thanks to the generosity of the De Medicis, Cosimo the Elder and then Lorenzo, both sons of Giovanni di Bicci, they started to rebuild the conventual church. At the end of 1438, Brother John arrived in Florence and set to work on the embellishment of the convent. He was to rediscover himself under the direction and encouragement of St. Antoninus, who was prior there from 1439 to 1444 and who made him the conventual syndic.[1]

On January 6, 1443, the church of St. Mark was consecrated by a papal legate of Pope Eugene IV, who had just held the Council of Union with the Greeks in Florence. The Mass was celebrated by the Pope himself, who so appreciated the Dominican painter that he called him to Rome to work at St. Peter's and at the beginning of 1446 even proposed to give him the Archbishopric of Florence. It was Fra Angelico who, tendering his refusal, suggested the name of St. Antoninus.

At this time Brother John was living in Rome and working in the Vatican on the chapel of St. Peter in the basilica and in the papal palaces. He was at the service of Nicholas V, who had been elected in 1447 in the very place where Fra Angelico was living, in the

[1] The conventual syndic or procurator took charge of the material needs of the religious and of the Priory in which they lived. Originally, St. Dominic wanted only the cooperator brothers to fulfill this role, so that the priests could devote themselves entirely to preaching. But the priests protested with such vigor that St. Dominic agreed to reverse his decision.

convent of the Minerva. After an interlude in Orvieto, where he decorated the cathedral with the assistance of Benozzo Gozzoli (1420–97), he was recalled to Fiesole, where the prior, his own brother Benedetto, had been stricken with a serious illness. After Benedetto's death, Brother John succeeded him from 1450 to 1452. He was then recalled to Rome in 1453 by Cardinal John of Torquemada (1388–1468), the great ecclesiologist, not to be confused with his famous nephew Thomas, Grand Inquisitor of Spain. Torquemada asked Fra Angelico to decorate the cloister of the Minerva, a work he did not have time to finish before his death on February 18, 1455. Those who are familiar with Rome know that he was buried in this church of the Minerva and that he still rests there, not far from St. Catherine of Siena, who left her impression on the entire Dominican spiritual renewal of the fifteenth century, enduring far beyond her death.

Fra Angelico of Fiesole thus stands at the crossroads leading in many directions in what was a transition period. It was a time of transition in the history of Western civilization when, due to a certain loss of medieval values, at least in Italy, the first outlines of humanism were emerging. It was a transition period in the history of Italian painting, set as it was between a Giotto (+ 1337), still very close to the art of icons, representing with magnificence and wisdom the popular Christianity embodied in St. Francis, and the arrival of the more tormented, sensual painting of the Renaissance. It was a turning point in the history of the Church, coming after the trauma of the Great Schism, with its three concurrent claimants to the papacy, a scandal to all and especially to the little ones—a period in which the papacy needed to win back its badly damaged prestige. It was equally a period of transition between Latin West and Byzantine East. A precarious union had been achieved at the Council of Florence, only to be followed by the great shock of the fall of Constantinople to the Turks in 1453, bringing about the definitive separation between East and West. Finally, it was a period of transition in the Dominican Order, where institutional unity, damaged by the two obediences,[2] needed to be reestablished, along with the need implied by the spiritual reform and reform of observance undertaken by Raymond of Capua, confessor and confidant of St. Catherine of Siena. Fra Angelico was situated in the full stream of this current and assumed the tasks of government and service of the common life in the Dominican Order while at the same time placing his genius at the disposal of a badly needed renewal of evangelical preaching, through the beauty of his painting. It is not going too far to emphasize the fact that art was,

[2] In the wake of the ecclesiastical splintering that the Great Schism caused, religious orders frequently experienced organizational divisions among their members. Indeed, even future saints were to be found in different camps, each group claiming allegiance to one or another of the claimants to the papacy. Each side, moreover, developed its own governmental structure, so that there were two Dominican Masters General. This phenomenon is called the "two obediences".

for him, the prime medium of preaching, and that his painting should still be seen in this light.

Fra Angelico was not perhaps the greatest painter of his time. He has been reproached for not having given sufficient place in his painting to the tragic dimension of wounded man, of the drama of the world, as some of his contemporaries did, for example, Masaccio (+ 1428) in his celebrated frescoes in the Brancacci chapel. Father Régamey, a specialist in sacred art, judged that Brother John "held himself aloof from the most recent, most impetuous currents" of his age. According to him, Fra Angelico bore witness to a fugitive moment of balance corresponding to the Florentine peace of the second third of the fourteenth century. But this moment proved as precarious as the Western Church's union with the Eastern Church. A ray of grace![3]

But art historians seem to set aside this somewhat severe judgment and prefer another interpretation of Fra Angelico's painting and his famous light radiating from color, in view of his theological vision. An art historian such as G. A. Argan has attempted to express it by speaking of "a sacral humanity".

The Proclamation of the Gospel Mystery through Beauty

Many attempts have already been made, at various levels and with different capacities, to show how the

[3] See *Portrait spirituel du chrétien* (Paris, 1963), p. 135.

Dominican artist's painting coheres with the vision of St. Thomas Aquinas. I can simply suggest here that his painting is inseparable from the vision of a world redeemed, that it tries and succeeds in showing that since the coming of Christ nothing can be truly seen, through faith, without the one who is the Creator and Redeemer of creation. His painting never ceases to speak of the Incarnation, manifesting a renewed order in the world that is expressed by light. Finally, it accords an exceptional place to the Virgin Mary, seen as the model of the creature living in perfect friendship with God in the midst of the joys and sufferings that mark salvation history.

The Light of the Incarnation and the Redemption

One of the rare recorded utterances of Fra Angelico, coming down to us by way of Vasari, concerns his own relationship with Christ. In his words, "To paint the things of Christ, one must live with Christ." So we can understand why on the walls of San Marco's cells and on its walls throughout, Fra Angelico associates St. Dominic familiarly with the events of Christ's life and especially his Passion. We notice too how often he depicts St. Dominic in a position suggestive of one or another of the *Nine Ways of Prayer*. In a widely known scene that adorns the residences and rooms of Dominican friars and sisters is the detail from the *Mocking of Christ* wherein St. Dominic sits absorbed in reading the Passion narrative, peaceful and recollected (Eighth Way). We see him with hands joined in the *Deposition from the Cross* (Fifth Way) or standing, his left hand uplifted (Fourth Way) or in the scene of the *Crucifixion* kneeling with both arms raised as he grasps the beam of the Cross. Fra Angelico could hardly indicate more clearly the participation of body and spirit in the sacrifice of Christ.

The body indeed has its role in this configuration of closeness to Christ. But Fra Angelico's bodies, in comparison with naturalism's, have a quality of luminosity, somewhat as in biblical exegesis the spirit is distinguished from the letter while remaining rooted in and dependent upon it. It is the painter's way of presenting, through an astute artistic disproportion, the spiritual reality he wishes to make clear.

On this topic, it has been remarked recently[4] that there are whole sections of abstract painting in Fra Angelico. We see this in the multicolored patches, somewhat like spatterings without formal design, that render nonrepresentational art five centuries before its theory and practice were developed. And is not another facet of abstraction, that is, abstraction's distancing from the factual, seen in the reverent handling of his figures' clothing, which is so suggestive of the unearthly?

Thus Fra Angelico works subtly by contrasting one part of a painting, marked by symmetry and harmony

[4] Georges Didi-Huberman, *Fra Angelico, Dissemblance et Figuration* (Paris: Flammarion, 1991).

(an effect of his Thomistic theology so aware of order in creation, as expressed in his flowers and trees) with another part executed in the quick strokes of abstract art. To us and our contemporaries, the absence of perspective, of a sense of depth in Fra Angelico's painting, is surprising, but this lack is replaced by light and color and gives at the same time a sense of strangeness, of otherworldliness. This effect is achieved by alternating somber and light planes and above all by the omnipresence of white. Although some of his figures remain stereotypical, for the most part this Dominican painter joins the spiritual quality of the icon with a highly aesthetic visual statement about human individuals.

His bringing together the two aspects of the Paschal Mystery, death and Resurrection, Cross and glory, produces a similar precious blend that belongs properly to theology. What the twelfth-century crucifix of San Damiano, so dear to St. Francis of Assisi, achieved by the representation of the *Christus Victor* above the inscription of the Cross, Fra Angelico conveys by the peace radiating not only from the persons surrounding the Cross but also from the Crucified himself. Even the *Pieta* of the Alte-Pinakothek of Munich, painted by Angelico about 1438, wherein the Virgin kisses the hand of her dead Son as they lay him in the tomb, is a work stamped with absolute serenity. Fra Angelico's concept of the Virgin inspires him to portray not only a human being who has entered into divine friendship but the very one who welcomed into herself the true Word of God.

The Virgin of the Annunciation

Like many Italian painters, Fra Angelico had a predilection for depicting the Annunciation, which is the scenario for the *Sacra Conversatio*, the holy dialogue between the Angel Gabriel and the Virgin Mary. Through the medium of this familiar scene, he is able to bring alive Mary's readiness to accede to the mystery, inclining more toward the word of God to be received than toward the heavenly messenger. The painter sows his surface with symbols. In the cloister corridor of San Marco, for example, the seemingly insignificant details of red and white flowers in the meadow of this Annunciation scene evoke the whole exegesis of the Song of Songs. In the same register as this dexterous play, the figure of the Virgin is far too large when measured against the actual physical proportions of the house, as if to show that she herself is the true House, the Holy Temple. So also the detail of the Virgin's robes, her white tunic covered softly by a black mantle, most unusual in iconography and strongly suggestive of the Dominican habit. In other frescoes of the Virgin at San Marco, her mantle is gray-violet over a red tunic, colors of sorrow and martyrdom.

In all the Annunciation scenes, the Virgin is seated or kneeling, her hands crossed upon her breast, inclining forward, scarcely less than in the scene of her coronation by Christ in glory,[5] as if to show that it is really the same mystery. Even the setting in this

[5] Cell no. 9.

Annunciation scene lends itself to the mystery of the
Incarnation—I would almost say in a cinematographic
mode—for in the background there is a door opening onto the unknown. In fact, in another Annunciation scene by Fra Angelico, the *Armadia degli Argenti*,
painted at the end of his life (1450), the door opens
onto a central aperture through which we see a series
of further doors, the whole completed by an idealized
setting of cypress and palm trees.

In this panel (p. 83), an angel with brightly col-
ored wings like those of a great butterfly addresses the
Virgin, whose garments, by contrast, are painted in
hues limpid and soft. A dove hovers over the scene.
The impression given by the play of delicate tones is
truly that of spiritual light, an inner radiance emanat-
ing from the Virgin, who is "filled with grace". In an
altar tableau by Fra Angelico entitled *The Annunciation
of Cortona*, the Virgin is wearing a blue mantle and a
red robe; further back hangs a curtain of that same red,
but higher, above the housetop, a panoply of stars!

Can art bring salvation? Will beauty save the world,
as Dostoyevsky believed? The answer has to be in the
negative. The beautiful can enrapture but not convert,
transport but not transform. Only Christ can do this.
But faith can discover Christ in every authentic experience. If, therefore, profane beauty can lead us along
the path of spiritual perceptiveness, how much more
sacred art! In both these areas Dominicans endowed
with artistic gifts have sought to preach in their own
medium. Their patron is Blessed Fra Angelico, but

they could invoke as well Blessed Andrew Abellon (1375–1470), prior of Saint-Maximin and manuscript illuminist, or Blessed James of Ulm (1407–91), master of the art of stained glass, or even Fra Bartholomew della Porta (1472–1517), who, while living at San Marco, must have pondered his predecessor's masterwork. These placed their talent at the service of proclaiming the Word Incarnate, which Word, in their hands, becomes again enfleshed. In the way of Fra Angelico, the Dominican vocation should lead us to discern the invisible through the visible. For our life includes the dimension of beauty to be discovered or fashioned in all that we do, in all that we sing, and in all that we preach.

Fra Angelico, *Annunciation*, Florence (Marzeri Schio,
Ed., Labergerie, Paris).

FROM THE OFFICE OF READINGS
FOR THE DOMINICAN VOTIVE OFFICE OF
THE SUFFERING OF OUR LORD JESUS CHRIST

A reading from a sermon on the book of Ezekiel by
Brother Girolamo Savonarola, priest (Ed. Naz.: *Pre-diche sopra Ezechiele*, a cura di R. Ridolfi, vol. II,
Rome, 1955, pp. 336–44)

Our True Love Is Christ Crucified

We are gathered here to contemplate the Passion of
our Lord and Savior: I do not know whether we ought
to be happy or sad. We ought to be happy because of
so great a salvation but to be sad because of such a
death. Let us therefore go in each direction; let us not
talk about anything other than love, as we all cry out:
love, love!

Our preaching will be refined and not refined, yet
everyone can receive it, particularly those who are
skilled in love. Those who are not skilled will know
their distance from love. Love has no order, so that we
may speak with the beloved and with Love himself. I
am not going to extend myself beyond the arrange-ment of the Passion, but you will understand me. Let
us all be attentive and enter into love.

Thinking about what I was going to say concerning
the Passion of the Lord, I saw a beautiful and well-dressed woman crying. Coming up to her, I said,
"Whom do you seek? Why are you crying?" The

spouse of Christ responded and said, "I am seeking my beloved, who will bring me peace. *I desire him whom I love.* I not only desire him and his love, but I desire nothing else from him except that love." *I found the watchmen in the land*, that is to say, the poor apostles, *and I asked them and said*, "Whom do you love?" "We certainly love Love. Behold, let us show you the crucified Christ: he is our true love. O, how this Crucified One is Love itself!" He is indeed. And so I grasped him, and I said, "Are you love?" He responded, "*I am the man who has seen poverty.*" O, why are you poor? "Because love is always poor: love forgets everything else, except for the thing beloved. I was very rich, and now I have become poor; I used to have everything, and now I seem to have nothing. And so I would wish that you could forget everything, and I would want to make you love with me, and we would be one love together."

Truly, you have all the conditions of loving, O Lord Jesus. Truly, you are true love. I gaze upon your hands, feet, head, your holy mouth, and your whole body, and you are all love. But can you not redeem human nature without this kind of suffering? "Of course I can, since every act of mine is infinite; but love wants not only this but even greater things. Therefore I, the Son and Eternal Truth, ought to bring it about that I should seem to die among you." But could this not be otherwise? "Absolutely, it could be; but the divine command *surrounded me*, and love would not permit otherwise. Love *has shackled my feet in chains*, binding me in prison, and holding me. A small suffering is given to others, but all suffering is given to me."

What do you say, Mary, fruit of the love of the beloved? Do you not wonder about this great love? O Virgin, what do you say? "*My beloved is radiant* because of his divinity, *and ruddy* because of his humanity. He is chosen above all the angels, because he is love. *His words distill like the first myrrh*, that is the first mortification, and the first passion: therefore I, my son, was content with regard the rational part."

O love, are you still not satisfied, having been condemned in this way by men? Was what you had not sufficient for you? The Cross was placed upon his shoulders, between two thieves, but love bore all things. Along the way, he came to the Virgin (according to some). Seeing her Son with her own eyes, and the Son seeing his Mother, the glance became an embrace: "O my Son, what is this?" "Mother, *it is fitting that this should happen for salvation*."

They came to the mount. Love was not neglectful. He prayed; "Father, behold: love has led me thus far. Behold, my flesh; behold, my sacrifice. *They have pierced my hands and my feet*, and I offer myself for all of the Jews and for all of those present and to come." When he had said this, he offered himself freely. He stretched out his hand, and it was nailed. The other hand was taken, and his feet as well. O Lord Jesus, what is this? O heavens! O angels, O Mary, what are you doing? Behold! The Cross of our Lord and God!

Behold love, dearly beloved friends. O divine Love, how can I see you except as a consoler? You became a curse: everyone mocked you, and you were standing, O Jesus, and you said, *Spare them.* You said, *I thirst,* and you became drunk with gall. Love has thus led me. *Remember,* O my soul, *my poverty.* Here is your King and your God. I commend this people to you, O Lord. Through the love of your inmost self, spare this your people, O Lord. Amen.

Responsory   Lam 1:12

℟. All of you who pass by, behold and see, * If there is any sorrow like unto my sorrow.

℣. Behold, all you people, and see my pain. * If there is any sorrow like unto my sorrow.

6

LAS CASAS AND
THE STRUGGLE FOR JUSTICE

Father Bartolomé, thank you for this support
In the dark hours of the night ...
At the highest pitch of agony
You give hope.

A CROSS THE CENTURIES, transcending beliefs, the
Chilean poet Pablo Neruda, so deeply involved
in politics himself, has rendered this homage to the
impassioned Dominican whose voice was raised in
the sixteenth century against the decimation of South
American Indians, against the pillage of the first
colonization.

A Progressive Conversion

Nothing in the first part of the life of Bartolomé de
Las Casas could have hinted at a vocation to fight for
justice or could have aroused in him that virtue of zeal

that he placed in the service of peace. Born in 1484, he came from a family with a taste for adventure, which was fully satisfied, for his father and uncles sailed with Christopher Columbus on his second trip, resulting in the definitive colonization of Hispaniola, that island now divided between Haiti and Santo Domingo. Las Casas himself attempted the long voyage, and if he was in 1512 the first priest to be ordained in the New World, he remained no less blind than others to the desolation that colonization brings in its train when unhampered by scruples.

If we can believe it—it has been strongly contested—the figures furnished by the "Very Brief Account of the Destruction of the Indies" drawn up by Las Casas in 1552 reveal a horrendous decimation of populations. About the islands of San Juan and Jamaica he wrote, "There were more than six hundred thousand people on the two islands, perhaps more than a million. Today there are only two hundred left on each island. All these Indians perished without religion, deprived of the sacraments."

With a few exceptions, there were no massacres. But the colonists demanded labor far beyond the strength of an extremely undernourished population. Mining decimated the natives, mistakenly called Indians (because Columbus thought he had reached the Indies), for they were employed in mining the gold and silver for which the Spaniards were so avid.

In Cuba, where he was established after Hispaniola, Las Casas was no worse an *encomendero* than the others, even though he passed for a priest who was attached to the goods of this world and firmly determined to retain them. He did not question the legitimacy of the system, the injustice, the misconstruction of Queen Isabella of Castile's intentions as we can see them in her last Testament of 1504, and of the declarations of the Popes, who wished to promote the evangelization of the New World.

One Sunday toward the end of 1511, however, a voice cried out "in the desert", that of a Dominican, Antonio of Montesinos, who did not mince words, as Las Casas reports them: "You are in a state of mortal sin, and you will die in it, because of your cruelty to an innocent race."[1] The charge was electric. All the colonists, who believed themselves good Christians, saw themselves excluded from the sacrament of penance—so crucial at a time when their lives were in constant danger—for refusing to free their slaves. Indeed, one day that charge hit Las Casas himself. The incident caused him to reflect. Shortly after, the shock of witnessing a bloody slaughter brought him to the point of conversion.[2] He realized the injustice of a situation he had profited by. To the amazement of his friends, in 1514 Las Casas the priest-colonist gave the Indians all he had gained through their work in his mines and embarked for Spain with Montesinos. From this time on Las Casas was to spend his life in the service of the Indians, fighting for them. He went to plead their cause with the Spanish Cardinal, the

[1] *Historia de Las Indias*, III, chap. 4, BAE v. 96, p. 176.
[2] Ibid., III, chap. 29, BAE, v. 96, p. 244.

celebrated Franciscan Cisneros, regent of the kingdom of Castile, who granted him the official title "Protector of the Indians". But the New World was so far from Mother Spain!

Five thousand miles: a round trip might take up to fifteen months because of navigation by convoys for which one must wait; and there were other causes of delay as well. His plan was to gather Hispanic-Indian communities together under the direction of religious at Cumana (northeast of what is today Venezuela). Peasants from Castile and elsewhere would come to teach agricultural techniques to the Indians and would live with them in peace. But let a shipwreck come, or a drunken revolt, and the idealist's project was undone by cupidity and egoism. His recruits were interested not in winning souls, only in getting rich!

There was a second error, which history has been careful to record. In 1516, when presenting his plans for reform, Las Casas proposed to import black slaves to be used for the work. In view of this, the attempt has been made to implicate him in the slave trade. In fact, however, he had been misinformed about the manner in which these Africans had been enslaved by Islam. And Las Casas bitterly regretted this ill-conceived idea, writing later in his "History of the Indies": "I can never be sure that this ignorance of mine is really an adequate excuse for me before the judgment seat of God."[3] But have there not been

[3] III, chaps., 102 and 129; BAE v. 96, pp. 417 and 487b.

many saints in history who committed grave faults of which they repented? Still, this fault has slowed up his canonization process considerably.

After this setback of error in judgment, Las Casas withdrew into silence for twelve years. He joined the Dominicans in 1522 and prepared himself by study and prayer for a new combat: a second conversion ensued. From 1531 on, with great prudence and at the same time vehemently and with increasing indignation, he seized every opportunity to make the voice of justice heard. He was constantly engaged in this activity on all fronts, philosophical and theological as well as legislative and administrative, and with a growing intransigence that earned him the denunciation of a Spanish historian, Menendez Pidal, for his "pathological passion for leveling accusations".

Tenacity and Indignation

The first thing to be done was to convince his opponents—a task for an intellectual. A simple but basic question had to be addressed: Were the Indians by nature free beings? Las Casas had to grapple with an obscure text in Aristotle's *Politics* that referred to "natural slaves". Commentators, imbued with the paganizing Renaissance viewpoint, believed this could be applied to the Indians in the New World. Las Casas had already been confronted in one of the new American dioceses by a bishop who held this strange theory. But in 1550 he had to pit his strength against a redoubtable adversary, Sepulveda, a canon of Cordoba and a translator of Aristotle. Las Casas, in a lengthy *Apologia*, only recently published, refuted his opponent's arguments point by point, demonstrating that the Indians could not be included in Aristotle's category.

Once admitted, therefore, into the human community, the Indians had to be protected. In memoranda, reports to public authorities, and entreaties to the Council for the Indies, Las Casas never ceased to point out that the Indians had been, and still were, the victims of a twofold violence: not only that which had subjected them by force, and illegally, at the time of the Conquest, but also the economic and social domination that had followed.

When, at the request of the Dominicans in the New World, Pope Paul III published his bull *Sublimis Deus* in 1537, Las Casas composed a long commentary on it that he first had circulated in a manuscript: *De unico modo . . .*, that is, "On the one way of leading the entire human race to the Faith". This one way was simply nothing less than charity; there was no other way. We should note that these texts were composed during the era of a Pizzaro, with his brutal capture of the empire of the Incas.

In 1542 Las Casas obtained from Emperor Charles V the "new laws" that decreed that no further sale of Indians would be allowed and that all former transactions should be gradually terminated. As official texts did not cease to repeat, slavery was abolished, but it still remained to render this effective in actual fact and in the popular opinion. Although the Emperor had tempered their application, the "new laws" were accepted with very bad grace by the Spanish colonists, who detested Las Casas, who had won protection for the Indians from the public authorities. In the following year Las Casas was named bishop of Chiapas, an immense diocese now divided between Mexico and Guatemala, extending from the Atlantic to the Pacific.

In this territory entrusted to his care, Las Casas planned to build for "his" Indians a more durable structure based on gospel principles. After his experience with Cumana, Las Casas acted with the greatest prudence, both directly and behind the scene. Whatever the embellishments of the legend, unmasked by the more critical recent historiography, Las Casas was in truth the builder. More often than not he worked out of Spain, for he believed that in this way his beautiful work of peaceful evangelization would meet with greater success. Within a few years a country peopled by very aggressive tribes, called for this reason "the Land of War", was transformed into "the Land of True Peace" (*Vera Paz*). A gradual penetration, without recourse to arms, without colonists, achieved through the mediation of Indians already converted, with the aid of catechesis timed to the rhythm and way of life of the natives, had led to a truly peaceful evangelization. This Christian social experiment calls to mind the famous Jesuit missions in Paraguay in the seventeenth century, short lived in fact, and may be seen as an original model, a first experiment.

Named to the Council for the Indies in 1543, Las Casas never returned to America after 1547, judging that the closer he was to the authorities, the more useful he would be. He never ceased writing tracts, exhorting, convincing, and driving the authorities to action. His tone grew ever more urgent, eager, full of the fire that characterized his zeal. These lines taken from the preface to his "Very Brief Account of the Destruction of the Indians", composed in 1540 and printed in 1551, gives us an idea of it. He is addressing the future Philip II.

> I have lived fifty years and more in these great realms, better, in this vast New World of the Indies, bestowed and entrusted by God and his Church to the Kings of Castile to direct and govern in their name, both temporally and spiritually, so as to lead them to conversion and hope. And I have witnessed injustice and abuse, exactions and brutality beyond all human imagining.... Since these actions are in themselves evil, tyrannical, detestable, and condemnable by all standards of natural, human, and divine law, I have resolved to publicize them, lest by my silence I be responsible for the loss of innumerable souls and bodies occasioned by the tyrants.

We see therefore that it was his own conscience that goaded Las Casas into writing and bearing witness to injustice. This is why he wrote his monumental "History of the Indies", which was published only after his death. As an old man, we see him in the grip of final "doubts". Certainly the slaves must be freed, protected, welcomed into peaceful lands, but after the bloody conquest of Peru was it not necessary to go still further? A Christian, according to him, was in duty bound to give back to the Indians what had been taken from them. Las Casas' recommendations to confessors enjoined that at the moment of death a colonist should be required to give up everything he had unjustly acquired. And without regard for compromise, or, it must be said, for realism, the Dominican wrote, "The Catholic King of Castile, our sovereign, is obliged, under pain of damnation, to restore the kingdoms of Peru to the Inca, grandson of Guainacapac." The famous treasure of the Incas should likewise be restored to him. Concerning the legitimacy of the Spanish conquest, his Dominican contemporary, Francisco de Vitoria, a professor at Salamanca, was to find a solution based on law and theology, which would in fact be more constructive than all the legal proceedings launched by Las Casas against the colonizers.

One feels that the protector of the Indians was stirred to the very depths of his heart. In his last letter, dated 1566 and addressed to Pope Pius V, who was himself a Dominican, Las Casas pleaded once more, "In the newly Christianized lands, let priests give back all the gold, silver, and precious stones that have come into their possession, for they have taken them from men who suffer the most dire want and continue to live in misery." The letter was never finished. Las Casas died in the midst of this final struggle.

Las Casas does not represent the totality of the Dominican mission in Latin America in the middle of the sixteenth century. There were St. Louis Bertrand and Jerome of Loasia; there was also the extraordinary missionary work carried on by the religious Orders, which risks being overlooked because of the clamor of our Bartolomeo, still resounding in our ears. How can we forget the symbol of Christianization represented by the Virgin's gift to poor Juan Diego, her own image depicted on the fragile material of his tilma? A small Aztec hieroglyphic on Mary's robe symbolizes the winning over of the ancient religion to that of the true God. For this is what the first account of the miracle of Guadalupe affirmed. The Virgin asked that a sanctuary be built, so that her Son, Redeemer of the world, "might be revealed, exalted, and given to men in this place".

But he must be made known in all the purity of the New Covenant, and it was precisely this truth that Las Casas had to proclaim. Without justice, he said, it is impossible to preach the Faith. Using very strong words, he cried out, "The Indians have come to hate the true God himself, because it was in the guise of men preaching him, and preaching faith in him, that so many calamities have fallen upon them."

Las Casas was simply expressing in his forceful way the two convictions underlying the Christian mission. The evangelizer must speak with the voice of friendship and persuasion, and the one who hears the word must accept it freely. For at bottom, this is what it is all about: the fight for justice for the Indians is also a fight for their freedom. This freedom belongs by right to every man created in the image of God and ransomed by him. Aristotle's reference notwithstanding, the importance of establishing the freedom of the Indians is clear. "When in doubt about a person's freedom," said Las Casas, "we have to lean toward the side of liberty, for after life itself, this is man's most precious gift."

The most modern aspect of Las Casas' personality is his personal involvement. When all confrontation and dialogue with their oppressors failed, he was ready to lay his life on the line, in solidarity with these Indians whom he saw as suffering members of Christ even though not yet baptized. This explains the blazing words he addressed to his brothers in the episcopate: "The bishops of the Indies are obliged by divine precept to plead with the Emperor insistently, even at the cost of their lives if need be, to deliver the Indians from oppression and restore their former freedom."

This vision is modern and universal, but Las Casas, despite his fiery language, rejected all violence in his fight for justice. He simply wanted to witness to Christ, who came to save all peoples. But he was convinced that his vocation as a Friar Preacher could not be lived out in terms of merely abstract and theoretic theology. In his life story, human drama resounds through the centuries, down to our own day. Las Casas had received the gift of zealous indignation. Did he not write to the future Philip II in 1545, "I believe God wants me to fill heaven and earth, and the whole earth anew, with cries, tears, and groans!"?

From a letter written to the Order from the General Chapter of 1255 by Blessed Humbert of Romans, priest and fourth Master of the Order (*Ep.* 3: *Opera de vita regulari*, ed. J.-J. Berthier, vol. II, Rome, 1889, pp. 492–94)

Woe to Us If We Depart from the Path of the Apostles

I make known to your charity that, among the numerous desires of my heart raised up by reason of the governance I have received, there is one that is great indeed: it is that by the ministry of our Order schismatic Christians may be called back to the unity of the Church, and the name of our Lord Jesus Christ may be carried to the Jews, Saracens, pagans, barbarians, and all the nations, so that we may be his witnesses and the cause of salvation for all men *even to the ends of the earth.*

But two obstacles stand in the way of this result.

One of these is the failure to know languages; hardly any brother wishes to devote himself to their acquisition, and many prefer to probe all sorts of curiosities rather than to learn something of use.

The other is the love of one's homeland, whose sweetness has embraced many whose nature has not yet been transformed by grace, to the extent that they *do not wish to leave their country or their family or forget their nation.* Instead, they want to live and die in the midst of their relatives and friends, and they are not at all concerned that among these the Savior *could not be found even by his own mother.*

Wake up, brothers called by God, and see whether there are such examples from the apostles. *Were they not all Galileans?* And which of them stayed in Galilee? Did not one journey to India, another to Ethiopia, another to Asia, another to Greece? Did not all of them, spread about in distant lands, thus produce fruit in the world that we still see?

If someone were to say that these things were quite important, but we are too weak to be able to imitate them, then woe to us if we want to be preachers and stray from the footsteps of these preachers! More than that, did our early fathers speak in these sorts of terms, the men whom our Holy Father Saint Dominic sent throughout the world, novices as well as others? Let not such a base thought arise in our hearts, we who are chosen by God; but, attentive to the call of our profession and to the glorious reward of prompt obedience, let us lay ourselves open to anything in order to spread the salvation of souls and the glory of the Savior!

If someone, under the inspiration of God's grace and according to the will of his superior, finds his heart ready to learn Arabic, Hebrew, Greek, or any other language from which he will be able to produce some good result in his apostolic labor at an opportune moment; or, if someone finds himself disposed to strike camp in his own country in order to enter the province of the Holy Land or of Greece, or one of the others close to the infidel, and which need brethren who would be ready to endure a great deal for the Order, for the Faith, for the salvation of souls, and for the name of our Lord Jesus Christ, then I beg and exhort him not to fail to write to me and tell me of his state of mind about this.

I commend you, each and every one, to the kindness of the Savior and his most glorious Mother, our advocate, whose protection has most certainly helped our Order, particularly in these days, and been of great use to it.

Given in Milan, at the General Chapter, in the year 1255.

Responsory   Ps 97:2, 3c; 110:9

℟. The Lord has made known his salvation; in the sight of the nations he has revealed his justice, * And all the ends of the earth have seen the salvation of our God.

℣. The Lord has sent redemption to his people. * And all the ends of the earth have seen the salvation of our God.

7

SAINT CATHERINE DE RICCI
AND THE MYSTICAL DIMENSION
OF THE DOMINICAN LIFE

IN OUR ORDER a mystical dimension developed in
various parts of Europe in a succession of waves,
each one generating the next, as it were. There was
the Rhineland school of the thirteenth century, with
Meister Eckhart and his disciples among both friars and
sisters. There was an Italian school deriving from St.
Catherine of Siena, which through Savonarola continued its influence to the end of the sixteenth century.
There was a Spanish school, also with Savonarolian

The quotations in this chapter are taken from the French translation
of the Letters of St. Catherine de Ricci, made by "a sister of the Third
Order Regular of St. Dominic" (Paris, n.d., ca. 1895) (L.). This text
was based on the first Italian edition: *Le Lettere spirituali e familiari di
Santa Catarina de' Ricci*, raccolte e illustrate da Cesare Guasti, Florence,
1890 (G.). There is now a critical edition of the Correspondence:
Santa Catarina de' Ricci, *Epistolario*, ed. G. Di Agresti, 5 vols., Florence, 1973–75.

influence, which became eremitical in the sixteenth and seventeenth centuries with Louis of Granada and had effect in South America, in St. Rose of Lima (+ 1617), for example, and later in France in Louis Chardon (+ 1651) and Alexander Piny (+ 1709).

The selection of St. Catherine de Ricci (1522–90) as an example of Dominican mysticism is not made easy for the reason that what made her mystical life so admirable to our predecessors was the extraordinary and miraculous. From contemporary biographical accounts such as the anonymous *Apologia*, or the *Lives* written during her lifetime by Nicolas d'Alessi, or that of Seraphim Razzi written in 1594, we read steadily of the apparitions of Christ crucified and Christ risen, of weekly ecstasies between 1542 and 1554, and of the stigmata—stigmata that have been received both before and after Catherine de Ricci by such friends of God as Francis of Assisi and Catherine of Siena.

But through it all, St. Catherine de Ricci appears as a remarkable example of the mystical life at a period of thoroughgoing Church reform, determined upon by the Council of Trent and prepared for by the Savonarolian movement. The monastery where Catherine resided, St. Vincent's in Prato, was founded by disciples of Savonarola in 1503 as Third Order Regular, and Catherine had been cured through her intercessory prayer to Savonarola on several occasions, notably during a terrible illness in 1539. It needs to be remembered that at this point in the sixteenth century the Tuscan scene in which Catherine was situated was riddled with intrigues, plots, battles, and political rivalries.

Finally—and most remarkable of all—there is the spiritual and moral balance of this saint's life, which contrasts with the spectacular element of the signs she received, signs that sometimes interfered with her desire for peace and tranquility in the daily life of the community. Catherine, opposed to the curiosity and taste for the marvelous in her regard, begged the Lord "to deliver" her from the outward show of these supernatural signs. "In your kindness, my Jesus, deliver me from all these visible manifestations ... so that my poor monastery may retrieve a little of its contemplative and tranquil spirit", was her prayer.

Among the great saints this contrast between what seem to us extraordinary forms of the mystical life and the serenity accompanying daily decisions is not uncommon. We think of the tears of St. Ignatius and his meticulous care in governing the Society, or the ecstasies of St. Teresa of Avila and the practical common sense with which she established her foundations, to take two examples from St. Catherine's own time.

Between 1552 and 1590 she was prioress seven times, with the intervals prescribed by law; during those intervals she filled the charge of subprioress with a regularity that is well known even today. On more than one occasion she affirmed that the burden of governing weighed her down, was a martyrdom for her. This is easy to believe. She had to deal with many problems and was obliged to confide the interests of the monastery to lay "trustees" who had to be informed of her business and above all tactfully handled if they were generously inclined. She had to keep in touch with the authorities in Prato and Florence (the Medicis), with the authorities in the Dominican Order—the Master of the Order and the Provincial of the Roman province—and with the local ordinary. She had to deal with difficulties in her own family, reconciling, making peace "in a world where everything is turned upside down".[1]

During all this time, every week from noon on Thursday until four on Friday afternoon, for twelve years, she was deprived of the use of her senses. She received in her flesh the wounds of Christ, temporarily from 1538 and then in a permanent way from 1542 on; they were first visible, later hidden. She saw embedded in the index finger of her left hand a red circle, which became a sort of ring, a sign of her mystical marriage with Christ, which had been concluded on Easter morning 1542, and she wore the crown of thorns. In addition, there were the numerous illnesses that often tried her.

How was she able to reconcile these two spheres of activity? On the one hand she moved on an exceptional, extraordinary plane whose authenticity some of her Dominican brethren, always rational, doubted and wanted to test; on the other hand there was the daily round of current business, necessary, often banal, sometimes tiresome.

[1] Letter of Feb. 13, 1588, to L. Capponi (L. 305 G. 328).

On the feast of Corpus Christi, June 6, 1541, Catherine received the gift of permanent union with God in the highest point of her soul, so to speak, while her sensible soul retained its natural activity. She was given a heart like to that of the Virgin Mary, "attracted and drawn by God—which is beyond all power to conceive—and was led into the true paradise", says the anonymous *Apologia*. Moreover, her spirit remained full of joy and serenity.

What comes down to us from St. Catherine herself is a voluminous correspondence, consisting mainly in spiritual direction. In it we find much energy, common sense, realism, and especially an appeal to joyousness. There is nothing lugubrious about her, no wild or extravagant play of imagination, and in her letters she makes absolutely no allusion to her supernatural privileges and mystical trials. At most she occasionally mentions her great weariness.

Her Realism

We find this in her letters to her spiritual sons, especially Buenaccorso Buenaccorsi, a Florentine notary who served as procurator for the convent (+ 1555). She repeatedly urges him to have recourse to doctors and medicine for his health and not to multiply his fasts and privations during Lent: a man of the world should not live like a monk, but "each according to his own condition".[2] She tells him to keep the

[2] Letter of Dec. 28, 1552 (L. 117 G. 179).

commandments and not to be ungrateful to God, who has given him so many gifts, even if some days bring their difficulties, and to forgive his son Vincenzo, who has offended his father by incurring debts and keeping bad company. Mother Catherine is practical. "If I deserve to obtain this favor, and if you can with 150 crowns get him out of his trouble and pay his debt, it would make me very happy; I do not want to go against you or force you to do it, but it seems to me the boy is sincere. This arrangement would benefit all concerned."[3]

Another proof of her realism is the way in which she adapts her spiritual teaching to the capacities of her correspondents, her compatriots, who were for the most part bourgeois businessmen whom we picture as active and wealthy members of the Italian Renaissance period.

She often uses examples from the world of commerce, elsewhere inspired by the gospels. To these merchants, the Salviati, the Capponi, the Buenaccorsi, she speaks at the beginning of Lent about being "spiritual traders" eager to prosper, acquiring holy virtues and good will. "In the blessed Jerusalem everyone can be enriched by this torrent of treasures, even as we see all kinds of merchants gathering when a trade fair is advertised in some city ... for all graces pour down from heaven." She even goes so far as to speak of a "spiritual fair".[4] Catherine surely is thinking of the

[3] Feb. 5, 1582 (L. 151 G. 213).

[4] Mar. 29, 1555, to Buenaccorso (L. 13 G. 197).

daily business that she could witness from her monastery window; in European towns, such weekly fairs
are still common.

Her realism is also shown in the famous episode
regarding the enclosure. When the Council of Trent,
intending that the life of sisters should be truly ascetical, insisted on material enclosure, some of them
became preoccupied with implementing this in a
rather mechanical way. St. Catherine, being prioress in 1576, with all her desire for obedience to the
Church, the Pope, the Master of the Order, and the
Provincial, found herself involved in a rather compli-
cated affair. Through a misunderstanding, difficulties
arose in the daily life of convents, because of purely
practical contingencies, susceptibilities, and financial
necessities. She declared that whatever touched the
interests of the Order "touches the pupil of my right
eye". Catherine de Ricci was fully aware that the
Constitutions of the Third Order Regular permit-
ted the sisters to leave the enclosure "even though
our only reason for doing so is to beg". Therefore,
strictly speaking, the rigid law of enclosure did not
affect them, and she proposed, while redoubling the
admission that her own sins were the cause of all
the trouble, that the solution would be to wait, so
as to appease benefactors and religious who were
"overly stirred up" about the business. "Oh, my
Father," she said to the Provincial, "with patience
we can overcome everything."[5] You see that she was

[5] Letter of Mar. 6, 1577 (L. 4 G. 36).

caught between the wishes of her secular friends and those of the Provincial, but by holding to her rights, she succeeded in establishing the distinction between nuns and sisters.

Her Joy

The second characteristic to be found in St. Catherine's practical spirituality, one that is a part of her mysticism, is her insistence upon joy. It runs through her letters like a leitmotif. She reassures, she consoles, she counsels, but always enjoins, "Remain joyful."

She does not hesitate to write this to St. Philip Neri, great mystic though he was, favored with prolonged ecstasies, and still very humorous as well. "Live in joy, despite the thought of your last end." Recall that anguish over the question of salvation was the great preoccupation of the time.

She speaks of joy to everyone, even the great ones of her day. To the Duke of Urbino, terrified by the sudden death of his son-in-law, she writes, "One must surrender oneself joyously to God."[6] "We must be content with everything it pleases our Creator to ordain", she tells Ludovico Capponi[7]—which is the great and simple lesson for religious life above all. She is not lacking in humor in her letter to the very touchy Ludovico Capponi, that belligerent, elegant,

[6]C. Mar. 13, 1588 (L. 29 G. 318).
[7]June 6, 1575 (L. 260 G. 283).

and handsome gentleman whom she wants to convert, suggesting that he "allow his cause to take a little nap".[8] In other words, give your cause a break, or, with still greater familiarity, "Cool it!"

To Dianora Biffoli,[9] the wife of one of her spiritual sons, who had health problems, she writes at Christmas in between two thank-yous for jams and jellies, "I should like you to be joyous, for they tell me that you are very sad, and this is good for neither soul nor body: it is not the way to get better.... I beg you, my daughter, surrender yourself to Jesus more than you have done. If you love me even a little, be joyous." What abandon, what simplicity in this remark, and what natural and supernatural intuition! Catherine's balance and serenity are rooted in her intimacy with Christ in her mystical life.

If the Dominican mystic leaves us unenthusiastic, or perhaps frightens us because of her speculative heights or extraordinary manifestations, this may be because we fail to see the humanity, the realism, the joy with which Dominican saints took up their daily struggle. As Catherine put it serenely, strengthened as she was by prayer and purity of heart, "Sweetness and bitterness are always intermingled in this world, but this is the way we must walk, and it is enough that we are following in the way of salvation."[10]

[8] Aug. 26, 1574 (L. 254 G. 2779).
[9] Dec. 27, 1585 (L. 170 G. 136).
[10] Feb. 2, 1589, to Capponi.

From a letter to Buenaccorso Buenaccorsi from Saint Catherine de Ricci, written on Palm Sunday, April 18, 1554 (to Buenaccorso Buenaccorsi of Florence: *Epistolario*, ed. G. Di Agresti, vol. I, Florence, 1973, pp. 331–36)

We Found the Red and Ruddy Sign of Victory, Jesus on the Cross

Rivalry ought really to be thought of as a good. It is not envy, as if someone were to hold back his neighbor from the good, lest that person get there first. Rather by holy rivalry and a thirst for the heavenly spring we must hasten with great vigor; without an obstacle in anyone's way, we must strive to advance. Ah! if only this rivalry were in Christian hearts, how many people would come to that desired reward, which now only a few people are able to reach. My dearest son, *let us so strive that we may run and obtain it.* In this contest you will not be considered careless, just as the thief crucified with Jesus, even though he was unprepared, was judged to be not unhappy but rather happy. Does he not seem to you to have struggled far better than that great crowd of holy fathers who waited for their redemption in limbo for ages? For the thief, in an instant, swiftly ran to beat all the others and be worthy to be the first one at the victory, which he took away from none of those who were called to it.

Now indeed, my son, we live at a time in which running and taking a stand are more than we are used to doing. Considering the height of the mystery of our redemption, which is presented to us in these days, how much more should we stand firm and persevere!

First, we see the mercy that overcomes justice and is made the mediator with the eternal Father, which induces him to send his only Son to take on human flesh for the salvation of our souls in his immortal gift. God reaches down from heaven to earth, and *he whom the heavens are unable to contain* is confined in the Virgin's womb and became, from almighty God, a child like all of the rest of the wretched of the earth, from immortal and unable to suffer he became mortal and suffering, from divine he became human, from the wisest of all he became like a fool in the sight of men, from the Lord whom angels serve he became the servant of men.

What sort of mind, when considering these things, does not marvel that all of this was done so that human nature might pay the debt that it owed to the divine Essence? And because our nature was unable to discharge the debt, nor was it able to open the gate of heaven that disobedience had shut, behold the Savior came, rich with such treasure, ready and able to pay off the debt for us and to restore us as heirs of the heavenly estate. This consideration ought to restrain us in all of our activities, I mean those activities that are earthly and futile.

It is necessary that we run this race, roused up by the example of the abyss of the love of the Son of God toward his little creature. He ran his race together with our nature, so swiftly and to meet such a Passion.

And so, my son, we must run this race, and we must push ahead with strength toward that great open sea by which we are washed and cleansed. For our sake he did all this, and so we sign our foreheads with his sacred blood, so that we may approach the eternal Father with such a sign and we may tell him that his only begotten Son discharged our debt. We have competed and have found the red and ruddy trophy, which is Jesus on the Cross, sprinkled with blood and deathly pale in the cause of love.

Responsory   Mt 11:29–30

℞. Take my yoke upon you, says the Lord, and learn from me, for I am gentle and lowly of heart. * For my yoke is easy, and my burden is light.

℣. Come to me, all you who labor and are heavy burdened, and I will refresh you. * For my yoke is easy, and my burden is light.

8

SAINT MARTIN DE PORRES:
HUMILITY AND LOVE OF THE POOR

O N MAY 6, 1962, a few months before the cele-
bration of Vatican Council II, Pope John XXIII
proposed to the world a new model of sanctity when
he canonized a Dominican cooperator brother, a
mulatto black, Martin de Porres, who lived in the seventeenth century in Lima, Peru. He linked this event
with the very aim of the Council: "The renewal of
the Mystical Body of Christ, the Church, through the
one means possible, namely, sanctity". The next day,
greeting pilgrims from Peru, John XXIII stressed the
humility of the new saint, saying that Martin de Porres
was not an academic but possessed "the true science
that ennobles the spirit", "that light of discretion" of
which St. Catherine of Siena speaks.[1]

On the eve of this Council, in which learned
Dominican theologians like Father Chenu and Father

[1] Letter 213.

Congar, and many others besides, were to play a significant role, it was both paradoxical and useful to show how the Church, which has need of authentic intellectuals, looks first of all for holiness of attitude, the fruit of humility. It is true, we are inclined to attribute this virtue spontaneously to Franciscans, or if need be to Benedictines because of their Rule, rather than to Dominicans, who are accustomed to being in the spotlight and appearing before large audiences, and above all to speaking, and speaking a great deal. Talking is a thing we never refuse to do either in public or in private—but it is not necessarily the best way to cultivate humility. St. Benedict's ninth degree of humility states clearly, "Let the monk restrain his tongue from speech, remaining silent, saying nothing unless he is questioned, for Scripture tells us, 'Where there is much speaking, one cannot easily avoid sinning' (Prov 10:19)." And it must be admitted that in much speaking a person may, without willing it and even without being aware of it, reveal much pride and pile up rash and hasty judgments.

And yet Dominican Tradition is not silent about the need for humility. St. Martin de Porres must have been familiar with the famous "Testament" of St. Dominic, which he had every reason to believe was authentic. He was probably brought up on the three recommendations: "Have charity, guard humility, make your treasure out of voluntary poverty",[2] which

[2] Cf. art. Creytens, *AFP* 1973.

Peter Ferrand reports in his *Legenda*, and which may well have had some foundation in St. Dominic's own words. Moreover, the mention of humility frequently recurs in Jordan of Saxony's portrait of St. Dominic in the *Libellus*. He describes the young canon of Osma as shining like the evening star, the planet Venus, which is closest to the sun, "last in his humility of *heart*" (the emphasis is important), "first in his holiness",[3] and throughout his account he develops this aspect of the Founder's personality. The triad— poverty, charity, humility—is stressed by Jordan of Saxony in his spiritual letters to Diana d'Andalo,[4] and to them he opposes the three temptations of riches, delights, and honors.

Furthermore, a magnificent text of the Primitive Constitutions, portraying the master of novices,[5] gave the early brethren a description that surely fitted Dominic himself: "He teaches them humility of heart and body and tries to impress this point on the novices, according to this word: *Learn of me, for I am meek and humble of heart.*"[6] Following this, the redactor, who was perhaps Jordan, has added three of the degrees of humility contained in Chapter VII of the Rule of St. Benedict: frequent and sincere confession (this combines the first and fifth degrees), giving up one's own will (second degree), and willing obedience to the will

[3] No. 12.
[4] For example, Letter 15, ed. Walz, MOPH XXIII, p. 21.
[5] No. 13.
[6] Mt 11:29.

of the superior (third degree). The text then lists all those little details that make community life bearable and shows how to put humility into actual practice, for humility is nothing if it is not concrete.

While the Rule of St. Benedict speaks of *ascending* the degrees of humility, using Jacob's ladder as a symbol (chap. VII, for "one is lowered by lifting oneself up and one ascends by humility"), Jordan of Saxony substitutes a still more telling image. In the *Libellus*,[7] speaking of the early brethren and explaining how they adopted the customs of religious, St. Dominic's successor declares that "they proposed to descend through the degrees of humility".

To descend, to lower oneself, to cultivate humility of bearing and manner, but especially humility of heart: we see here the relationship between this virtue and poverty, that love and care of the poor that characterized St. Martin de Porres. We see here how Martin understood the holiness of Dominic and the ideal of the first brethren. In Martin's undertaking the lowliest of services to all, we see humility at work within the Church, the splendid place each person holds in the Body of Christ, the equality of all races. He points us toward unremitting service to the poor as the best translation of our own vow of poverty, or at the very least, the sign of its authenticity. All reason enough to evoke the moving image of this simple man who still radiates the gifts of God.

[7] No. 38.

St. Martin (1579–1639) spent nearly all of his long life in Lima, in colonial Peru, this dependent territory built upon the ruins of the empire of the Incas. Don Juan de Porres, a Castilian gentleman, knight of the Order of Alcantara, had two illegitimate children by a black woman, originally from Panama, Anna Velasquez. When on December 9, 1579, a black infant boy was born, his father refused to recognize him and abandoned the mother. Thus in little Martin's blood there flowed two historic destinies, two cultures, that of victorious Catholic Spain and that of the blacks deported to America for manual labor in this immense land to be exploited after the destruction of the Incas. His very skin bore the mark of the unprivileged of this time, but his swarthy face would come to radiate the light of charity.

This light began to shine very early, and all those around him were surprised at his generosity, reverence, and selflessness, qualities rare in a child. We know that, marveling at his developing intelligence, his father eventually recognized him as his legitimate child, seeing to his education and giving him a trade, that of a barber, which in those days meant also an infirmarian and, if need be, a surgeon. At the age of fifteen he presented himself at the Convent of the Holy Rosary in Lima and asked to be admitted as a tertiary in the service of the community. His father and the superiors would have preferred him to be a lay brother, but he chose the humbler position. In point of fact, he became a cooperator brother with solemn vows in 1603.

From accounts of his life in the Convent of the Rosary, we can see how closely he resembled St. Dominic, whose image he had in his poor cell, together with one of the Blessed Virgin and a Cross. He too had no bed until they obliged him to; he too offered himself "to be sold" to pay the convent debts; he had the same desire to be a missionary—he wanted to go and evangelize the Far East: to each his own Cuman Tartars. Witnesses have assured us that he had a certain gift of bilocation, for people met him in all parts of the world, although he never left Lima. He is the saint of remarkable travels.

St. Martin de Porres had a burning love for the poor, whom he cared for and fed all day long, in a very practical way and under very difficult circumstances at times; he had astounding gifts of healing and of prayer. He whipped himself or had himself beaten by others in a frightening way; his fasting was practically continual. He was the kind of saint seventeenth-century Spain was very fond of, but first and foremost he radiated charity and humility.

Sayings have been attributed to him that are outstanding for common sense as well as supernatural sense, a characteristic of saints. One day the prior of the convent reproached him for having carried a sick Indian into his own cell, thus being disobedient. After accepting his penance, Martin replied, "I did not know that the precept of obedience came before that of charity." On another occasion, being reprimanded for putting a very dirty beggar in his own bed, he rejoined, "Compassion is better than cleanliness. For bedding can be washed, but floods of tears cannot wipe out the fault of hardheartedness toward an unfortunate person." Such was the wisdom of St. Martin, who did not hesitate to arbitrate a discussion between two student brothers about the essence and existence of God, citing St. Thomas Aquinas, for, as the regent of studies remarked on this occasion, he had "the science of the saints". But for himself personally it meant that the demon, who is so proud, was tormenting him grossly, because he was only a poor laybrother, senseless and ignorant.

All these anecdotes, these marvelous and miraculous stories, are found in a small biography written in 1671 by Father Bernard of Medina,[8] which is based on the testimonies given at the process introduced by the Congregation of Rites in 1668, and especially on a companion of the last four years of Martin's life, a certain Juan Vasquez. He attests to a charity grounded in humility that was truly captivating, extending even to animals, and always rooted in humility. Being a mulatto and a laybrother exposed him to many humiliations in the society of his time, even from the brethren. But he showed a strong respect for his brothers, seeing them as men of the Eucharist. "I am so grateful to him", he said of a Dominican priest who had insulted him, "that I would kiss, not his hands in which God descends to us each day, but his feet,

[8] *Vida prodigiosa* ... (Lima, 1673; Madrid, 1675).

touching them only with fear and veneration, for they are those of a minister of God."

One could multiply admirable incidents and prodigies in a life that would have little value for a historian but that a believer can see as wholly devoted to the service of God and others. In truth, this Lima of the early seventeenth century witnessed, beneath Martin's Dominican habit, an amazing convergence of the charisms of prayer, silence, humility, and service of the poor. Martin de Porres knew the young Juan Macias well (1585–1645), the young Spanish shepherd who crossed the Atlantic and also became a laybrother in the other Dominican convent in Lima, dedicated to St. Mary Magdalen. Juan Macias, in his porter's lodge, organized social welfare for an army of poor people. It is also probable that Martin knew Isabel de Flores, Rose of Lima (1586–1617), even though she was a semi-recluse in her parents' garden. This young Dominican tertiary had as her spiritual director Juan de Lorenzana, Provincial of Peru, the one who had received St. Martin into the Order of Preachers.

This constellation in the one city of Lima in the early seventeenth century is truly astounding: three Dominican mystics devoted to the service of the poor, interceding for the salvation of the mixed society that surrounded them, in which the desire to live and to become rich as quickly as possible reigned supreme. In contrast, they themselves lived intensely their relationship to Christ and to his Body. All three recognized in the grace of Dominic a way of dedicating themselves to the salvation of the world through heroic humility. Calling them to mind is a way of reminding ourselves that our engagements in the service of all the good causes in the world, all that we do, all that we say, will find a deeper echo and credibility if they are marked with the humble awareness of our poverty, which we take so much trouble to hide.

From the *Dialogues* of Saint Catherine of Siena (chapter 7, ff. 10v–11: Trad. Lat. Ms T. I, 4, Bibliotheca communalis of Siena)

On the Variety of Gifts in the Church

The soul in love with my truth never ceases to be of service in a small enough way to all the world, in common and in general.

Later on, the soul obtains an advantage on account of the union of love that it has with me. Blessed with this unitive love, it reaches out in longing charity to the whole world's need for salvation, joining this to the soul's own needs. This happens at the very beginning from the conception of the virtues, from which the soul drew the life of grace, whereby it fixes its attention on the particular needs of its neighbors. While it did this first in general, as was mentioned before, out of the desire of love for every rational creature, the soul then joined at length specific needs according to the number of different graces I have given to the soul for distribution. To some I concede the virtue of teaching, that is, of the word, giving sincere and upright counsel to one's neighbor; to another I give the example of life: everyone ought to do this, edifying their neighbors by the best possible instruction of a holy and upright life.

These are the virtues, with innumerable others, that are brought to birth in love of neighbor. I have made them different, because I did not wish to display all of them in one person alone.

I give this person one virtue and that person another. Although all the virtues are connected to each other, and it is impossible to have one without the rest, still I give them in different ways so that one virtue might be, as it were, the source of all the others. To one person I give charity as the primary virtue, to another justice, to another humility, to another a living faith, to another prudence, temperance, or patience, and to another courage.

And so these and many other virtues, in a spiritual and corporeal fashion, are distributed differently to different souls. I say in a corporeal fashion because of those things that are necessary for human life: I have bestowed the rest in such a great diffusion that I have never given all of them to one person, so that by force of this you may have a reason to exercise charity to one another.

I could have very well supplied all men with everything they needed for the body and the soul, but I wanted to make each one dependent on his neighbor, that each of you might be a steward to distribute the goods and graces that you had received from me. Thus, either willing or unwilling, man cannot escape from the exercise of the force of charity toward one's neighbor. Nevertheless, unless such an act is done for love of me, it will avail him nothing as far as grace is concerned.

Responsory   Cf. 1 Cor 1:9; Gal 3:28

℞. Blessed be the God and Father of all, who has called us into the fellowship of his Son, our Lord Jesus Christ, * For he is Lord of all.

℣. For there is neither Jew nor Greek, slave nor free, * For he is Lord of all.

9

LACORDAIRE, OR
THE DEFENSE OF LIBERTY

THERE ARE MANY INTERPRETATIONS of the word *liberty*: political, economic, philosophical, and also religious, just as there are many possible uses of these liberties. In the middle of the nineteenth century, Henry Lacordaire, a young lawyer, then a diocesan priest in Paris, and finally the restorer of the Dominicans in France according to a concept that was to spread to the entire Order, wanted to Christianize this word *liberty*. At that time the word had a political and philosophical connotation that the Church could not accept, because it seemed to her to be linked with the French Revolution, which had destroyed the thousand-year-old social order and persecuted religion. It is not surprising that this term, used by Lacordaire, was a shock, coming from a priest so attached to the traditions of the Church and so obedient to the Holy See.

Henry Lacordaire was born in 1802, at the moment when the Empire of Napoleon I intended to take on the heritage of the French Revolution without toppling into anarchy, the better to conquer Europe. Losing his father by death, brought up religiously by his mother, the young Henry lost the Faith, like so many of his generation. He returned to "the source", however, what he understood as baptism, when, alone in Paris, he began his legal career. With characteristic ardor he immediately entered the seminary in 1824. After his studies in theology, he was ordained a priest, but found no ministry to challenge him or suit his taste. It was then that he thought of leaving France for the United States, land of liberty. Everything was arranged, and the Bishop of New York was awaiting his arrival when the Revolution of July 1830 struck in Paris, opening a period of hope.

With Lamennais, a renowned priest known for his intelligence, and Montalembert, a young noble who had rallied to the cause of liberty, he founded a daily newspaper, *L'Avenir*, which carried this proud motto: "God and liberty".

The three friends and their collaborators fought for freedom: freedom of the press, of association, of nations and local communities, and also freedom to teach. Without authorization—for the French state had a monopoly and was anticlerical—they opened a free school. They were condemned, but their voices had been heard. The ideas expressed in *L'Avenir* were condemned by Rome, and they all separated from

Lamennais, who was unwilling to submit. Lacordaire, however, did not give up his ideal of liberty. He was invited to preach at Notre-Dame, where sermons customarily focused on apologetics, and he met with enormous success. But in 1836, aware of his need for intellectual and spiritual deepening, he retired to Rome.

It was here that his idea of restoring the Dominican Order in France ripened. The Order had been suppressed, like the other Congregations, by the French Revolution. In a memoir that he addressed in March 1839 to "his country", that is, to public opinion in France, Lacordaire pleaded for a recognition of the citizens' right to association, which had been granted to all except religious. Having received the Dominican habit in Rome in April 1839 and made his novitiate, he returned to France. Now, clothed in the black-and-white habit that had not been seen in France for nearly half a century, he again took up his Conferences at Notre-Dame in February 1841. In spite of difficulties, he reestablished several Dominican convents in succession, and their number rapidly increased.

"An unrepentant liberal", as he called himself, after the Revolution of 1848, which established the Republic, Lacordaire was elected a deputy, but he resigned quickly, realizing the incompatibility of a religious vocation with the hazardous struggles of politics. In December 1852, after the coup d'etat that illegally created an authoritarian empire for Napoleon III, he withdrew from public life, considering with a sense

of pride that since he himself was "une liberté", that
is, a symbol of political liberty, he ought to "disappear with the other liberties". He devoted himself to
his work as Dominican Provincial and founded new
convents before calling upon his final resources for
the education of the young, creating schools whose
spirit and teaching methods were inspired by Catholic
principles.

To the very end, Lacordaire defended the con-
sequences of his "liberal Catholicism", such as the
separation of church and state, or his preference for
a papacy relieved of the temporal duties that fell to
the Church in Italy. He died on November 21, 1861.
On all fronts Lacordaire had championed liberty, with
one object deliberately pursued: the reconciliation
of the Church and the modern world as it issued from
the French Revolution of 1789. He judged this world,
and rightly, to be the world of the future. In this sense
he can be considered a precursor of Vatican II.

What Is Liberty?

Lacordaire, as we have seen, fought all his life for liberty, and for those concrete liberties without which
the word was meaningless. It is true that he did not
propose a "theology of liberty" properly so called, for
his was not a systematic mind, despite his efforts to
organize the Conferences of Notre-Dame in a frame-
work in view of their publication. It was due to this

limitation of his that we cannot find in his works any reflection on the social aspects of Christian liberty, which would have been so welcome in this nineteenth century of the industrial revolution. But Lacordaire did build up a kind of apologetics of liberty, deeply rooted in personal experience and the experience of the Church.

The Path to Inner Freedom

Lacordaire, like all his generation, was raised in independence of spirit and behavior: "Son of an age that knows nothing of obedience", he said of himself, "independence was the air I breathed, and all my motivation."[1] His conversion therefore took the form of a journey to inner freedom that led him to Christ. In 1846 at Notre-Dame, evoking this journey, he exclaimed, "I have reached the life whose fragrance I breathed in childhood, lost in adolescence, regained as a young man, which I adopt and proclaim to every creature now that I have come to maturity."[2] This life was made possible by a liberation first of the mind, then of the heart. This was what he tried to share with his contemporaries, especially in his preaching at Notre-Dame, "through a word of friendship, a word that gives more than it asks ... that proceeds wisely, letting in the light gently as one restores life

[1] Autobiographical note, p. 91.
[2] Conference 37, v. IV, p. 7.

to someone tenderly loved who is ill".[3] But what also must be touched was the heart, that profoundly biblical word so important to Augustine, Pascal, and Lacordaire as well, for it recurs constantly in his speech and writings.

The Liberating Church Must Herself Be Free

This personal conversion was rooted in a very clear awareness of belonging to the Church, for it was within the Church that his liberation was effected. Lacordaire said this very explicitly when he was led to distance himself from Lamennais' system and to judge it severely: "I have learned through my own experience that the Church is the liberator of the human spirit, and that out of liberty of mind all other freedoms flow inevitably. In this clear light I have seen the questions that divide the world today."[4] This is why the Church herself must be free, that she may be fully a place of liberty.

For the Church draws her interior strength from grace and divine institution and her external strength from liberty. He showed in 1835 at Notre-Dame[5] that grace is by its very nature free, and that fortified by this divine element, the Church rests upon her liberty. He summarizes the ecclesial reality as follows: "The

[3] Preface to the Conferences, v. II.
[4] V. VII, p. 161.
[5] Conference 6.

free preaching of the Gospel, the free offering of the Sacrifice and the free administration of the sacraments, the free practice of virtue and the free continuation of her hierarchy".

Lacordaire concluded from this that the Church should be separate from the state and that she could claim modern forms of liberty for herself and others, for she knew their source: "The Church ... recognizes that modern forms of liberty are the legitimate outcome of the freedom of the Middle Ages, whose original source lies in the holy gospel of Jesus Christ."[6] Pope John Paul II speaks in the same way regarding the rights of man, and we heard similar phrases when Cardinal Lustiger, Archbishop of Paris, commented on the motto of the French Revolution on the occasion of the bicentenary of 1789.

Pleading in 1839 for the recognition of the right of religious to assemble, pray, and live in common, Lacordaire believed that they were simply "claiming from France their share in the liberties which she had gained". The freedom to gather as friends of Jesus Christ is one of the inalienable rights of man.

Friendship, "the Sure Sign of Greatness of Soul"

There is in the thought of Lacordaire, and above all in his conduct, a great insistence upon friendship, sympathy, the exchange of sincere sentiments, which

[6] Letter to Mme. de la Tour du Pin, 1, 39.

are rooted in his unceasing quest for liberty. Surely friendship is defined by free choice, free fidelity, the free search for a common good.

Lacordaire's correspondence reveals to what a point his entire existence revolved around friendship, the great preoccupation of his life. He talked about it at all stages of his life, never going back on it, never breaking a single friendship unless in the case of Lamennais, whom he looked on less as a friend than as a master with a strange personality. No word recurs more often in his letters than friendship, unless perhaps liberty, or heart, three spiritual realities totally bonded in his mind.

There were the friendships of his childhood and youth, and to these he remained faithful. One was Prosper Lorain or Théophile Foisset, who was to write the only biography that is still indispensable today. Then during the *L'Avenir* period there was his friendship, never exclusive but always impassioned, with Montalembert, eight years his junior; Montalembert was an aristocrat, Lacordaire was a commoner; Montalembert a layman, Lacordaire already a priest; Montalembert engaged, then married, Lacordaire vowed to celibacy. Lacordaire's expressions in his exchanges with Montalembert come so close to the language of love that it demonstrates an enormous amount of candor and of purity to have the courage to use them. But here we are in the full tide of romanticism, and what is more, Lacordaire understood perfectly the spiritual and psychological dimensions of his friendship: "I find in you alone the sum of all the strengths I have been given for other affections which I shall never know."

Lacordaire is enunciating a great principle here: "There are not two loves, one for creatures and one that joins us to God; it is only that this last is infinite."[7] This is the reason for his great friendship with Madame Swetchine, based on reciprocal admiration but with a touch of veneration on Lacordaire's side and an attentive and maternal protectiveness that were part of her Russian soul. On Madame Swetchine's side, this friendship was lived out entirely under the gaze of God.

Light is thrown on this concept of friendship by the admirable pages found in a small occasional work, a Panegyric of St. Mary Magdalen, written by Lacordaire in 1860, one year before his death. He wrote it to launch a fundraising campaign for the restoration of the Convent of St. Maximin. Mary Magdalen, Martha, and Lazarus, who according to Tradition came to Provence, were friends of the Lord Jesus. Their home in Bethany was one where he loved to come for a meal and to rest as with a family. With this as his point of departure, Lacordaire describes the beauty of Christian friendship and links it clearly with freedom. "Friendship is the most perfect of human sentiments because it is the most free, the most pure, and the most profound." And he continues, comparing it with the sentiments of conjugal love, or family ties: "Based on

[7] Letters to young people.

beauty of soul, it springs up in more free, more pure, and more profound regions than any other affection.... It is born in a movement of supreme liberty, and this liberty lasts to the end. ... Friendship lives of its own accord and by itself alone; free in its origin, it remains so throughout." Then he adds another beautiful definition: "Friendship becomes the reciprocal possession of two persons, ever free to part yet never parting."

Jesus Christ did not create friendship, "but he has given us back the secret of it", for it was lost, buried under sin. Thus in the context of salvation freely offered and freely accepted, he calls us not servants but friends. Thus, we have the example of Lacordaire to remind us of this Christian vocation to liberty and to show us the luminous way of living it out: to befriend our times, for he took it as a grace he had received, to be able to "understand his age"; to befriend those whom we encounter, but always in the name of our primordial friendship with Jesus Christ, whose name the preacher never ceases to proclaim: Jesus!

Let me end by recalling a beautiful expression that Lacordaire used during one of his Conferences at Notre-Dame. On this occasion, he departed from his prepared text, and in a moment when the grace of the word touched his soul deeply, he cried out, "Jesus, Jesus, your name alone has the power to rend my heart and to draw forth these words that burn within me and that, until this moment, I did not know!"[8]

[8] Conference 39, 1846.

From the *Treatise on the Re-establishment of the Order of Preachers in France* by Brother Henri-Dominique Lacordaire, priest (*Mémoire pour le rétablissement en France de l'Ordre des Frères Prêcheurs*, Paris, 1839, cap. III–V)

Dominic Was the Gardener of Christ

In the thirteenth century the Faith was very deep in all men. The Church still ruled a society that she had conquered for herself. However, the mind of European nations, which had been slowly worked on by time and by Christianity, was nearing the crisis of adolescence. The vision that Innocent III had seen in a dream—a church falling—St. Dominic revealed throughout the world. When everyone believed that the Church was Queen and Mistress, he declared that nothing less than a resurrection of the primitive life of the apostles could save her. Disciples followed St. Dominic as they once had Peter the Hermit: as many had become crusaders, now they became preachers.

All the universities of Europe contributed their masters and students. Brother Jordan of Saxony, the second Master of the Order, gave the habit to more than a thousand men whom he had drawn to this new kind of life. In an instant, or, to speak literally—for here truth surpasses metaphor—in five years, St.

Dominic, who, before Honorius' bull had only sixteen collaborators, eight Frenchmen, seven Spaniards, and one Englishman, founded sixty convents filled with chosen men and strong youths.

All of them, after the example of their master, wanted to be poor at a time when the Church was rich, poor even to the point of begging. All of them, following their Father, at a time when the Church was ruling, wanted to exercise only one kind of influence: the free surrender of men's minds to their virtues. They did not say, like the heretics, "The Church must be stripped bare." Instead they stripped her in their own persons and showed her to the people pure as she was at first.

They loved God, they loved him truly, they loved him above all else, and they loved their neighbor as themselves and more than themselves. They had received in their hearts the ample wound that has made all men eloquent. In addition to this was the merit of a burning soul, without which no one has ever been an orator. The Friars Preachers also had great skill in grasping what kind of preaching was suited to their time.

I shall mention by name some of those whom no oblivion will ever destroy. Among those in the thirteenth century was St. Hyacinth, apostle of the north, whose path we can follow by the monasteries he founded on his journeys. St. Peter of Verona was felled by the assassin's sword after a long apostolic career; with the blood that flowed from his wounds he wrote the first words of the Apostles' Creed in the sand: "I believe in God." In the fourteenth century, Henry Suso, a lovable man from Swabia, preached with such success that his enemies put a price on his head. During the same period, Brother John Tauler was acclaimed in Cologne and throughout the whole of Germany.

Let me add St. Vincent Ferrer, who, in the fifteenth century, evangelized Spain, France, Italy, Germany, England, Scotland, and Ireland; and Girolamo Savonarola, who was burned alive in the midst of an ungrateful people but to no effect, since his virtue and his glory rose higher than the flames at the stake. Pope Paul III declared that he would regard as suspect of heresy anyone who dared to accuse Savonarola.

I also add Thomas Aquinas, who quickly became the Catholic Church's most famous Doctor. There is also Brother Angelico, about whom Michaelangelo said that no one could paint figures like these unless he had first seen them in heaven. There are also Bartolomé de Las Casas and many others.

Let those who know them and call upon them guard these names, and let us end our summary of this huge Order with the words in which, in the fourteenth century, one of the greatest of Christian poets, the most celebrated singer of the *Divine Comedy*, sang its praises:

He was called *Dominic*, and I call him the gardener whom Christ chose to help him in his garden. He poured forth, like a stream from a lofty spring, his teaching and will and apostolic life. From that stream flow many brooks, by which the garden of the Catholic Faith is watered.

Responsory

℞. Grant us, O Lord, we beseech you, the remission of our faults: and, with the saints, whose solemnity we celebrate today as our intercessors, give us a devotion like theirs, * So that we may be made worthy to arrive in their company.

℣. May their merits aid us, who are weighed down by our own sins; may their intercession shelter us, whose actions accuse us: and may you, who granted to them the garland of heavenly triumph, not refuse us the forgiveness of our sins, * So that we may be made worthy to arrive in their company.

CONCLUSION:
SAINT DOMINIC AND FERVOR

IN SOME OF OUR CONVENTUAL CHURCHES and, by reason of history's vicissitudes, in certain museums now,
one can see what could be called a Dominican Jesse
Tree, a genealogical table of the holy members who
have issued from St. Dominic. Usually St. Dominic is
at the bottom of the painting or fresco, reclining side-
ways, somewhat like Adam asleep as his companion,
Eve, our mother, emerges from his side—for better or
for worse. From St. Dominic's side springs up a tree
whose branches space out vertically and whose leaves,
amid the flowers and fruits, image saints and blesseds
of the Order of Preachers. A variant of this concept
can be seen in the border at the base of Fra Angelico's
large Crucifixion scene in the chapter room of San
Marco. There the issue is like a great creeper, loop-
ing to the right and to the left of St. Dominic, which
bears seventeen medallions where we find two Popes
(Innocent V and Benedict XI), three cardinals, three
bishops, one of whom is St. Albert, and eight friars.
Surrounding them are nine figures of Old Testament
prophets as if to indicate that, apostle-like, the Good
News of Christ's death and Resurrection continues to
be prophetically preached by the Dominican Order.

There is nothing original about this representation, but it does convey the idea of the Founder's fruitfulness. Dominic is the trunk, the stock of the vine, the vine stock. As the Letter to the Romans[1] puts it, "If the root is holy, so are the branches." St. Dominic is the "Patriarch" of whom Gregory IX spoke in the bull of canonization, who would "beget", according to the expression of St. Paul to the Corinthians,[2] "a great number of sons devoting themselves with wonderful zeal to an evangelical ministry". In this text of July 3, 1234, the Pope drew a parallel between Dominic and the prophets, predecessors of the Founder of the Preachers. After eight centuries of Dominican life, with its glories and trials, we can see how the paternal figure of St. Dominic contains in germ different types of holiness that have been actualized in the course of history.

It is not difficult to reread the life of St. Dominic in the light of those who have rendered the Dominican charism more explicit. In Jordan of Saxony, in his building Dominican communion, we can see St. Dominic's concern for the sisters, first at Prouille, then at St. Sixtus, and also in Madrid in that brief handwritten letter that has come down to us. He established a very concrete relationship of collaboration between friars and nuns, while carefully preserving as much autonomy as possible for the latter. We recall

[1] 11:16.
[2] 1 Cor 4:15.

the reminiscences of Sr. Cecilia about the gathering of brethren and nuns for refreshment. After a lengthy conference Dominic had given "so that they might know what the Order was about". They all drank wine together from a cup that was passed first by Brother Roger among the twenty-five friars present, then by Sr. Nubia to the 104 sisters.[3] The master's care to implement his teaching with this joyous Dominican communion constantly calls us to meditation on the order's charism.

Although St. Peter of Verona, as we have seen, exercised a ministry of safeguarding the Faith—the word is not too strong to designate an Inquisitor—a ministry that St. Dominic was obviously unable to exercise, we can find in the Founder the same desire to convert souls and proclaim the true Faith. In this connection we recall the two notes, doubtless form letters, signed by his hand and destined to reconcile repentant Catharists officially. He had therefore an explicit mission in the Church to bring heretics back to the Faith, and he exercised it also with the Waldensians, whose errors were of a different kind. Dominic played a very important part in the reintegration of a section of the Waldensian movement, those who became what we call the Poor Catholics. But when recourse was had to arms, Dominic remained in prayer. Acting on the intuition of a saint, his only arms were "the armor of light". Like Peter

[3] Sr. Cecilia, 6.

of Verona, he was attacked by heretics. We know the incident of the heretical guide who led Dominic and his companions by thorny paths until their bare feet bled—reported by Gerard de Frachet.[4] Jordan of Saxony in his *Libellus* also recounts the story of an ambush in Albigensian territory into which Dominic, suspecting it was there, walked "joyously, singing aloud". Having escaped several times from such attempts to capture him, he lamented, saying, "I am not worthy of the glory of martyrdom; I have not yet merited such a death."[5]

For St. Dominic the preaching of Catholic truth had to be based on profound and continual study; St. Thomas Aquinas is the most apt example of this. Dominic at Palencia was "indefatigable at study", the *Libellus* tells us;[6] moreover, in applying to every young man the words of Jesus: "Blessed are those who hear the word of God and keep it",[7] Jordan is anticipating the Thomistic and Dominican motto: *contemplare et complata aliis tradere*. He comments, "There are two ways of keeping the divine word: one is to retain in our memory what we have heard; the other is to consecrate ourselves to it in deeds and show by our action the things we have heard ... the servant of God neglects neither of these." In Languedoc the missionaries sent back all their baggage except for their

[4] II, 2.
[5] *Libellus* 34.
[6] 7.
[7] Lk 11:28.

books "for the office, for study and disputation"[8]—the inauguration of an ascetical practice well known to all Dominican travelers, to have to carry along books that seem so heavy in railway stations and airports.

St. Dominic must have been a good theologian, since his treatise against the Catharists in the dispute at Fanjeaux was the best of all those prepared by the Catholics, and the fire that destroyed the writings of the heretics sent his flying out of the flames unharmed, "showing clearly both the truth of the Faith and the holiness of the one who had written it".[9]

As for a taste for study, we see St. Dominic cultivating ongoing formation long before it was discovered by modern pedagogy; he went with his companions to take a course in Toulouse under the celebrated master Alexander Stavensby.[10] In fact, we are able to reconstruct very precisely St. Dominic's preferences in scholastic matters; proof of it lies in his sending the Dominicans to various newly founded universities. This too evidences a very prudent apostolic option. We find further elements of the importance accorded to study in the Primitive Constitutions, in the texts on the student master. We read here of the wholly special solicitude given to students, who must be the object of his "attentive foresight".[11] The importance attached to study also explains the dispensation from

[8] *Libellus* 22.
[9] *Libellus* 25.
[10] *Legenda S. Dominici* (MOPH XVI, 400).
[11] Distinction II, XXVIII.

observances granted to professors and students and the magnanimity with which Dominic gave a private cell to those who would profit by it: "In the cells one may study, write, pray, sleep, and even stay up at night in order to study."[12]

A characteristic of Dominic's mission—being *in medio ecclesiae*—is clearly harmonized in St. Catherine of Siena, who learned from her Dominican brethren love of the Church and the grandeur of her service. The canonization document of 1234 names Dominic "teacher and minister in the Church militant". We see his dedication to the oneness of the Church in his preaching against heresy; to the universality of the Church in his sending the brethren "to far-flung corners of the Church of God";[13] to the apostolicity of the Church in his founding the Order "in imitation of the apostles" and in his attachment to Rome, the city of Peter and Paul; in the vision recounted by Constantius of Orvieto[14] and magnificently represented in the triptych of panels, now in the museum of Pisa. Dominic's concern to obtain from the papacy privileges and recommendations to help the Order to do its work better certainly indicated his lack of confidence in those bishops committed to the feudal system. Yet more than this, it shows his will for efficiency and readiness in fulfilling the Church's universal task. We recall the importance St. Catherine attached to

[12]Distinction II, XXIX.

[13]*Libellus* 62.

[14]*Libellus* 25.

the papacy, however compromised it may have been in the fourteenth century.

The texts coming down to us do not say whether Dominic was sensible to natural beauty and to art, so we do not know if Fra Angelico could have been inspired by his example. The sobriety of the texts brings out the contrast between Dominic and Francis of Assisi, who made poetry and admiration for creation one of the principal themes of his message. This is another reason why we deplore the absence of texts from the hand of St. Dominic, but I suspect that Dominic's art was the art of preaching "with his beautiful musical voice",[15] and that his grace was the grace of the word itself, for a homily can and should be a work of art. This must have been true of "the beautiful long homily" mentioned by Sr. Cecilia, which Dominic delivered to the sisters of St. Sixtus after having seen the Virgin Mary.[16] What we can say is that Dominic always showed that great sensibility common to artists and saints. This is proved by his tears during prayer and his compassion for every kind of suffering, as we know it from the depositions at the process of canonization.

The most moving episodes in the life of Dominic show him in accord with the intuition of Las Casas in the sixteenth century and his virtue of zeal. We need only recall his eagerness to share when he sold his books in Palencia—those books were truly

[15]Cecilia 15.
[16]Cecilia 7.

indispensable, as the chronicler makes very clear. Recall too his arrangements to set up a sort of welfare funding for the relief of the poor: "I cannot bear to study from dead skins when men are dying of hunger", quotes Brother Stephen, prior of Lombardy. Let us think too of the vehemence with which he tried to persuade the brethren to travel without money to their destinations. John of Navarre was reluctant to accede to this novel suggestion, and Stephen of Salagnac[17] describes Dominic "throwing himself at the feet of the disobedient friar, weeping and lamenting over the one who would not weep". Or again, we have his famous, ironic reflection on looking at the cells of St. Nicholas in Bologna, which had been constructed a bit higher than he had intended: "So you want to build palaces!" If historians have found Las Casas exaggerated, stubborn, and vehement, they might find similar qualities in the Founder of his Order, who went whole nights without sleep, who ate and drank little, and who burned with zeal for the gospel. His prayer sometimes burst forth with this fire, and in particularly dramatic moments he would stand upright, his arms in the form of a cross, "as if he wished to do violence to God by the sheer force of his prayer" (sixth way of prayer).

The mystical dimension in St. Dominic is basic. He did not take on exteriorly the rather frightening and extraordinary aspect of a St. Francis with his stigmata, or a St. Catherine of Siena, or a St. Catherine

[17] III, 8.

de Ricci. Indeed, he wore hairshirts discreetly; he was surprised in a state of levitation in the church of Castres,[18] and he possessed a well-attested gift of working miracles: the raising of the widow's son in Buvalisco from the dead and the nephew of Cardinal Stephen of Fossanova;[19] the multiplication of bread and wine.[20] But we note in him the same spiritual realism that struck us in St. Catherine de Ricci. He loved silent prayer, pilgrimages, the veneration of the saints and of relics,[21] all in perfect harmony with Catholic piety. The calm but unmistakable authority of St. Dominic, his decisiveness, his way of leading by example rather than words, and above all the remarkable balance of the institutions he founded all witness to the discreet audacity that characterized his sanctity. When he insisted to the brethren—even on his deathbed—on the prudence they should observe in dealing with women, or when we find in the Primitive Constitutions: "The brethren should not accept small gifts from women, nor give them",[22] is this a misogynist speaking, or rather his simple prudence and knowledge of the human heart, which in no way interfered with his affectionate treatment of the sisters?

We have already seen how much the humility of St. Martin de Porres owed to St. Dominic's inspiration.

[18] Salagnac I, 9.
[19] Cecilia 1 and 2.
[20] Cecilia 3 and 6.
[21] Salagnac I, 9.
[22] Distinction II, SSSVI, 7.

The first two ways of prayer are stamped with the sentiment of humility that completely possessed him. "I am not worthy": such was the meaning of his inclinations and prostrations, and above all the sign of veneration he taught the brethren to make before the crucifix, the sign of the humiliation of Jesus Christ, "so that Christ, who was so greatly humbled for us, should see us humbled before his exaltation". Jordan of Saxony speaks of the humility of his mind and heart, which he showed in childhood,[23] and this is of significant importance for a preacher who studies, confesses, and speaks. The great apostolic decision taken with Diego of Osma in Languedoc caused the legates of the Holy See to go forth with "signs of humility".[24] One of the most beautiful depositions of the process of canonization in Toulouse, that of Guillaume Peyre or Peyronnet, abbot of St. Paul in Narbonne, is filled with the impression of humility left by St. Dominic: "The witness never saw a man more humble in all respects ... he considered himself to be nothing ... he always wanted to wear poorer clothes than the other brothers." As for the ordinary folk questioned also at Toulouse, what struck them most was the determination with which Dominic refused the honors of the episcopate. If in St. Martin humility took the form of service of the poor, we can say that in St. Dominic it was a whole way of life, in perfect harmony with the end of the Order, with his prayer, his love,

[23] *Libellus*, 7.
[24] Frachet II, 2.

and his need for evangelical poverty, the living out of his contemplation of the word in the humility of the Incarnation and redemption.

We will not find in St. Dominic a plea for liberty; the term is modern and was so even for Lacordaire in the nineteenth century. However, St. Dominic's action was marked by the intrepid quality of Christian liberty. He did not allow himself to be deflected from his purpose, and others were aware of this spirit of liberty. This was clear when everyone opposed a decision he believed to be sound, such as the dispersion of the brethren on August 15, 1217. However, when—on rare occasions—he was convinced by opposing arguments put forward, he consented to withdraw from his original plan. This happened in regard to his proposal that the temporalities of the Order should be placed in the hands of the "*illiterati* laybrothers". The clerics "did not wish to be dominated by the laybrothers", and Dominic yielded.[25] Whether maintaining his decision or setting it aside, Dominic acted in Christian liberty for the common good and that of the apostolic ministry of preaching.

The clearest manifestation of this liberty in regard to the constraints we all experience (prejudice, antipathy, jealousy, envy) takes the form, in St. Dominic, of universal friendship. "He was kind to everyone," says John of Spain,[26] "to the rich, the poor, to Jews,

---

[25] John of Spain, deposition of Bologna, 26.
[26] No. 27.

infidels, so numerous in Spain ... he was loved by all." But this friendship was not distant; everyone who met him, without exception, felt him to be very close. Witnesses noted his special affection for religious; he loved to visit their houses and fall in with their customs. He placed his affectivity at the service of charity, and this must have attracted Jordan of Saxony, who was himself so attached to Henry of Cologne. "With his first glance, Dominic won all hearts", he tells us in the *Libellus*.[27] "During the day, no one was more sociable with his brethren or fellow travelers; no one more cheerful."

It is in a final passage[28] of the *Libellus* that we find the secret of Dominic, a text that indicates how he has been able to impart to his sons and daughters through the centuries ways to be developed and lived in consonance with their own times. Jordan speaks of "something more striking, something greater than the miracles"—an idea more modern than medieval. Jordan means Dominic's moral perfection and the impulse of divine fervor that transported him (*impetus divini fervoris*). St. Dominic bore witness by his fervor, the word *fervor* implying a kind of overflowing warmth, impetuosity. Here is the source of the realism of all Dominic's attitudes. It is said of him that he was intrepid, indefatigable; we admire his eagerness at study, at prayer, his zeal for the salvation of souls,

[27] 103.
[28] 103.

for peace, his desire to be a martyr, to travel ever farther afield proclaiming the word, his compassion, and above all his radiant joy in all circumstances, which astounded his companions.

Dominic must have loved the word *fervor*, since in the Primitive Constitutions he told the novice master to teach the novices what fervor they ought to show in their preaching when the time came for them to go out.[29] Jordan tells us that at the beginning of the Order Bishop Foulques of Toulouse rejoiced to see the exemplary religious life of Dominic and his brothers, the splendor of their grace, and their "fervor in preaching".[30]

The verb *ferveo*, rare in the New Testament, designates the fervor of the Spirit in Acts 18:25, as in Romans 12:9–1, where we find a summary of Dominic's life and teaching: "Let love be genuine; hate what is evil, hold fast to what is good; love one another with brotherly affection; outdo one another in showing honor. Never flag in zeal, be aglow with the Spirit, serve the Lord. Rejoice in your hope, be patient in tribulation, be constant in prayer." We can see how St. Dominic followed St. Paul here, as a mirror of perfection.

The seed of everything is contained in Dominic's fervor, and it is this dynamism that begets joy. This is the leaven that pervades Dominican life; it is the salt

[29] Distinction I, chap. XIII.
[30] *Libellus* 39.

that flavors all we do, the salt Christ asked of his apostles in the gospel. If we would have Jordan's concern for Dominican communion, if we would possess zeal for the Faith with Peter Martyr, if we would thirst to seek truth with St. Thomas Aquinas, if we are drawn to spiritual beauty and long to express it with Blessed Fra Angelico, if we love the Church like St. Catherine of Siena, if we struggle for justice like Las Casas, if we are aware of the mystical dimension of our life like St. Catherine de Ricci, if we desire humility in the service of the poor like St. Martin de Porres, and if we fight for the liberty of Christians and of the Church like Lacordaire—if we should do all these things and yet not have St. Dominic's fervor—we have yet to discover the essential. For I am convinced that beneath this "divine fervor", there lies hidden in him the fire of charity that enkindles the joy of the Spirit.

From the *Nine Ways of Prayer* of Saint Dominic, priest (Ed. I. Taurisano: *ASOP* 15, 1922, pp. 96–97, 99–100)

On the Prayer of Holy Father Dominic

The first way of prayer was to humble himself before the altar, as if Christ, whom the altar signifies, were really and personally present there, not just in a symbolic way. As it says in Judith, *the prayer of the humble and meek has always been pleasing to you.* The Canaanite woman obtained what she wanted by humility, and so did the prodigal son. Again it says, *I am not worthy that you should come under my roof,* because, *O Lord, I am utterly humbled before you.*

So our holy Father, standing with his body erect, would bow his head, looking humbly to Christ his Head, considering his own poor condition and the excellence of Christ, and giving himself completely to reverence for Christ. He taught the brethren to do this whenever they passed before a crucifix showing the humiliation of Christ, so that Christ, so greatly humbled for us, should see us humbled before his majesty. Similarly he ordered the brethren to bow in this way in honor of the whole Trinity, when "Glory be to the

Father, and to the Son, and to the Holy Spirit" was said solemnly.

After this, St. Dominic, whether before the altar or in the chapter room, would fix his gaze on the Crucified, looking intently at the Cross and kneeling down over and over again. Sometimes he would spend the whole night from the end of Compline until midnight kneeling down and standing up again, like the Apostle James, or the leper in the gospel who knelt down and said, "Lord, if you will, you can make me clean"; and like Stephen, who knelt and cried out with a loud voice, "Do not lay this sin against them."

There was great and increasing confidence from our holy Father Dominic in the mercy of God, both for himself and for all sinners, and for the protection of the novices whom he used to send to preach and win souls. Sometimes he could not contain his voice, but he was heard by the brethren to say, "To you, O Lord, will I cry: do not turn away from me, nor be silent before me", and other similar words from Sacred Scripture.

But also, at times, he spoke in his heart, and his voice could scarcely be heard. He would rest on his knees, his mind caught up in wonder, and this sometimes lasted a very long time. Sometimes, when he was like this, his gaze seemed to penetrate into heaven, and he would suddenly seem to be radiant with joy, wiping away the tears running down. He would be in great desire, like a thirsty man when he comes to a spring, or a pilgrim when he reaches his homeland at last.

He became stronger and more insistent, his movements always sure and orderly, as he stood up and knelt down over and over. He came to be so used to this kneeling, that when on a journey, either in the guest house, after the hardships of the trip, or on the road itself, when the others were sleeping and resting, he would turn to his genuflections as to his own special art, his own personal service. This he taught the brethren by his example more than by anything he said.

Responsory   Eph 4:15; Prov 4:18

℟. Doing the truth in love, * Let us grow up into him in all things, who is Christ, the Head.

℣. The path of the just is as the shining light, which shines more and more to the perfect day. * Let us grow up into him in all things, who is Christ, the Head.

POSTSCRIPT

Upon my return from the Dominican General Chapter held near Mexico City, I would like to place these meditations under the patronage of Nuestra Señora de Guadalupe. At the same time, I would like to express my gratitude to all those whose kind assistance made the publication of these pages possible: First of all, to Sister Mary Thomas Noble, O.P., of the Monastery in Buffalo, New York, for her generous service of translation that continues to express concretely the unity of mission among the sons and daughters of St. Dominic, to Father W. Becket Soule, O.P., for his refined English translations of the excerpts from the Dominican breviary, to Father John A. Farren, O.P., prior of the Dominican House of Studies, Washington, D.C., for his invitation to prepare these essays for the annual retreat, and to Father Joseph Fessio, S.J., without whose friendship and support my efforts to make St. Dominic known would be unavailable in English-speaking countries. Last but not least, I would like to express to Father Romanus Cessario, O.P. *toute ma gratitude et mon amitié*. To these friends all in Christ, I dedicate this book.

FR. GUY BEDOUELLE, O.P.
Fribourg

BIBLIOGRAPHY

For further reading in English:

Early Dominicans. Selected Writings, edited with an Introduction by Simon Tugwell, O.P. The Classics of Western Spirituality. New York: Paulist Press, 1982.

Benedict M. Ashley, O.P., *The Dominicans.* Collegeville, Minnesota: Liturgical Press, 1990.

Guy Bedouelle, O.P., *Saint Dominic: The Grace of the Word.* San Francisco: Ignatius Press, 1987.

William A. Hinnebusch, O.P., *The Dominicans: A Short History.* New York: Alba House, 1975.

Simon Tugwell, O.P. *The Way of the Preacher.* London: Darton, Longman and Todd, 1979.

Marie-Humbert Vicaire, O.P., *Saint Dominic and His Times.* Green Bay, Wisconsin: Alt Publishing Company, 1982.

Marie-Humbert Vicaire, O.P., *The Genius of Saint Dominic, A Collection of Study-Essays.* Nagpur, India: Dominican Publications, 1981.